VIK...
...204 N. Cascade
P.O. Box 717
Fergus Falls, MN 56537
(218) 739-5286

P9-APA-378

WITHDRAWN

LOOM
KNITTING
PATTERN BOOK

ISELA PHELPS

LOOM
KNITTING
PATTERN BOOK

ISELA PHELPS

St. Martin's Griffin
New York

This edition published by St. Martin's Press 2008.

All rights reserved. No part of this book may be used or reproduced in any manner whatsoever without written permission except in the case of brief quotations embodied in critical articles or reviews. For information, address
St. Martin's Press, 175 Fifth Avenue, New York NY 10010

www.stmartins.com

A Quintet Book. Copyright © 2008 Quintet Publishing Limited
QTT.LKB

No part of this publication may be reproduced, stored in a retrieval system, or transmitted in any form or by any means, electronic, mechanical, photocopying, recording or otherwise, without the prior written permission of the copyright holder.

This book was designed and produced by Quintet Publishing Limited, 6 Blundell Street London N7 9BH, UK

Art Director: Sofia Henry
Designer: Steve West
Photography: Jonny Thompson
Illustrator: Anthony Duke
Project Editor: Katy Bevan
Managing Editor: Donna Gregory
Assistant Editor: Robert Davies
Publisher: Gillian Laskier

Printed in China by 1010 Printing International Limited

Library of Congress Cataloging-in-Publication Data available upon request

ISBN-13: 978-0-312-38055-7
ISBN-10: 0-312-38055-0

First U.S. Edition: March 2008

10 9 8 7 6 5 4 3 2 1

Contents

Introduction

Hello dear friends,

We are pegging again! Loom knitting is hot right now, knitting looms are fast disappearing off the shelves and intrigued crafters are tapping into their creativity with the knitting looms. This book, like its predecessor *Loom Knitting Primer*, is here to help you with a little inspiration, to tap into your creativeness.

Loom knitting is the new "old method" to knit. Looms of all sorts and sizes are coming into the craft stores. You can find them in the regular circle shape, a long oblong shape, and even the new S shape. Do not let the shape fool you—it may look like a toy for your kids, but it is a great loom for knitting wide panels. You might say it is a toy for the kid in you.

Loom knitting is easy, fast, and full of possibilities. All it takes is a little yarn, 30 minutes of free time, and a loom, and you will be looming away in a cinch! No knitting experience is required... I promise. If you can open a can with a can opener, you can loom! It is all a matter of holding the yarn with one hand and wrapping it around the pegs of the loom, then with the knitting tool, you lift the loop on the peg and a stitch is created. Even stitches throughout, without the tension on your arms or strain on your hands. Come loom away with me, and you will be peggin' in no time!

In this book, the sequel to *Loom Knitting Primer*, I have brought you a collection of over 30 loom knitting patterns, by the best designers in the industry. You are sure to find a design that calls you and tempts you to grab the nearest knitting loom and break open that skein of yarn. The main portion of the book contains patterns for everyone in the family: from baby to even the furry creatures that love us. At the back of the book, you will find a quick refresher on loom knitting techniques, just in case you need a little reminder.

The designs included range from beginner to intermediate level; if you are craving a little lace, you will find it in here, if a cable is what your heart desires, you will find it in here too. Socks for everyone in the family, with a little lace and some cables, even some basic ones for those days when you just want to relax and knit. May you find inspiration within the pages of this book to create something spectacular.

Happy looming!

Isela Phelps

PART I
Tiny Tots

Little Travel Coat

by Isela Phelps

The design of this jacket brings a little glamour to the small tykes in our lives. Knit in super bulky weight yarn, this coat works up fairly fast. Choose contrasting color buttons to bring more attention to the front of the coat.

INTERMEDIATE

Materials

Knitting Loom

Large gauge knitting loom with at least 40 pegs [Sample used Yellow Knifty Knitter by Provo Craft]

Yarn

490 (500, 525) yds. [448, 457, 480 m] of bulky weight wool [Sample uses Rowan Big Wool, 100% merino wool, 3.5 oz (100 g) 87 yds. (79 m) in Ice Blue]

Tools

Knitting tool
Tapestry needle
Two buttons ½ ins. (1.3 cm) for smaller sizes, ¾ ins. (2 cm) for largest size

Size(s)

12–18 mos (2T, 4T)
[Sample shown in size 4T]

Gauge

10 sts and 13 rows to 4 ins. (10 cm)

Garter st

Row 1: K.
Row 2: P.
Repeat above 2 rows to create 1 garter st row (1 g-st ridge created).

Back

Cast on 32 (34, 40) sts.
Work in garter st for 4 rows (2 garter st ridges created).
*Next: K2, ssk, k to last 4sts, k2tog, k2.
Next: Work 4 (4, 6) rows in stockinette st (knit all rows)*.
Repeat from * to * 3 (3, 4) times.
Next: Work in stockinette st until item measures 7 (7½, 8) ins. [18, 19, 20.5 cm] from cast-on edge.

Armhole shaping

Next: Bind off 2sts at beg of next 2 rows.
Next: Work in stockinette st until armhole measures 5 (5¼, 5½) ins. [12.5, 13, 14 cm].
Next: Bind off all sts.

Left front side

Cast on 16 (17, 20) sts.
At the right side: the shoulder edge.
At the left side edge: the neckline edge. Maintain a garter st edge on the last 2 sts of this side. Work 4 rows in g st.

Size 12 and Size 2T

*Next row: K2, ssk, k to last 2sts, p2.
Next row: K.
Next row: K to last 2sts, p2.
Next row: K.
Next row: K to last 2sts, p2*.
Rep from * to *: 3 times (13sts remain, 14sts remain).

Size 4T

**Next row: K2, ssk, k to last 2sts, p2.
Next row: K.
Next row: K to last 2sts, p2.
Next row: K.
Next row: K to last 2sts, p2.
Next row: K.
Next row: K to last 2sts, p2**.

Rep from ** to ** 4 times (16 sts remain).
Work even until item measures 7 (7½, 8) ins. [18, 19, 20.5 cm] from cast-on edge (maintain the garter st edging on the inside edge).

Armhole shaping

Next row: (You should be at the right side of loom)—BO 2sts at beg of row.
Next: Work even for 7 (9, 11) rows.

Neckline shaping

Next row: Work to the end of row in established pattern.

Next row: BO 3 sts at neckline edge.

*Next row: K.

Next row: K to last 2sts at neckline edge, k2tog*.

Repeat from * to * until 8 (7, 6) sts remain.

Next: Work in St st until armhole measures 5 (5¼, 5½) ins. [12.5, 13, 14 cm].

Bind off all sts.

Right front side

Work as for left front, reverse all shaping i.e., BO for armhole at left side—on even rows, shape neckline on right side—all odd rows.

Sleeves

Cast on 16 (16, 18) sts.

Next: Work in g st for 4 rows.

Next: Inc 1 st at each end. 18 (18, 20) sts on loom.

Size 12 mos

Next: Inc 1 st at each end of every 5th row 3 times (24 sts total). 15 rows worked.

Next: Work 7 rows even.

Next: Bind off loosely.

Size 2T

Next: Work in stockinette st: Inc 1 st at each end of every 4th row, 5 times. (28 sts total) (20 rows worked).

Next: Work 4 rows even in stockinette st. (24 total rows worked for sleeve).

Next: Bind off all sts loosely.

Size 4T

Next: Inc 1 st at each end of every 4th row 4 times, then every 5th row once 28 sts total—21 rows worked.

Next: Work 5 rows even.

Next: Bind off loosely.

Neck Edging

Cast on 3 sts. Work a 3-st I-cord. Measure around the neckline and work an I-cord that is that specified measurement.

I-cord for button (make 2)

Cast on 3 sts. Work a 3-st I-cord for 8 rows. Bind off. Attach to the left side of coat. Position buttons on the opposite side.

Finishing

Block all pieces before assembly. Seam shoulders first. Sew sleeves, then join the sides and seam the underside of the sleeves. Attach I-cord button closures to the left side of coat. Position buttons on the opposite side. Sew the I-cord to neckline.

Animal Hat Trio

by Kathy Norris

These playful little animal hats create a smile on the face of the bear, bunny, and cat, as well as the face of your child!

INTERMEDIATE

Materials

Knitting Loom

Small gauge round knitting loom [Bear and bunny hats in small size uses youth hat loom. Cat hat in toddler size uses adult hat loom]

Yarn

103 yds (94 m) chunky weight for hat and ears; small amount of light worsted weight for face [Sample was knit using Louet Gems 100% merino wool bulky/chunky weight, 3½ oz (100 g) 103 yds. (94 m)
Bear – Sandalwood 44
Bunny – Champagne 01
Cat – Pewter 43
Duplicate st face – Louet Gems 100% merino wool light worsted weight, 3½ oz (100 g), 175 yds. (160 m) in black]

Tools

Knitting tool
Crochet hook
Tapestry needle

Size

6 months to 1 year (toddler)

Gauge

18 sts and 24 rows to 4 ins. (10 cm) in stockinette st

Pattern notes

Pattern was designed with cast on from right to left around the loom. Stockinette st – knit every row.

Hat body

Ch co pegs of hat loom.
Work stockinette st for 7½ ins. (8½ ins.) [19 cm, 21.5 cm].
Dec the crown by moving every other st to the next peg, and knit bottom loop over top.
BO using gather bind-off removal method.
Secure tails and trim excess.

Ear pattern for each animal hat is below. Knit as indicated.
To attach ears to all hats, lay hat flat. Place a pin at the both sides of the center of top of hat to mark the placement of ears.
For cat and bunny: Position ears at top of hat approximately 3 sts from center of top.
For bear: Position ears at top of hat approximately 5 sts from center of top.
For all: Use mattress st (p. 135) to seam ears all the way around the ear. Secure tail and trim excess.

Each animal face has a chart to follow. Using light worsted weight yarn and tapestry needle, embellish the hat by using duplicate st following the chart for each animal face. Center the face on the hat. Fold the hat so that the ears are touching, and place a pin to mark the center of face.

Bear Ears

(make 4 and st 2 ear pieces together for each ear).
Ch co 15.
Work stockinette st for 5 rows.
Beg at peg with working yarn attached:
Move loop to next peg with st. Bring bottom loop over top.
Repeat * to * until 1 loop (the one with working yarn) remains. K 1.
Cut yarn and pull tail through tightly forming a half circle.
St 2 ear pieces together along the arch of the half circle for each ear.
Attach ears to hat.

Bunny Ears (make 2)

Ch co 22.
*Sl 1, p9, k12.
Sl 1, k11, p10*.
Repeat * to * 9 more times.
Sl 1, p2tog, p5, p2tog, k2tog, k7, ssk, k1.
Sl 1, k9, p8.
Sl 1, p2tog, p3, p2tog, k2tog, k5, ssk, k1.
Sl 1, k7, p6.
Sl 1, p2tog, p1, p2tog, k2tog, k3, ssk, k1.
Sl 1, k5, p4.
Sl 1, p2tog, p1, k2tog, k1, ssk, k1.
Sl 1, k3, p2.
Sl 1, p2tog, k2tog, k2.
Sl 1, k2, p2.
Sc BO 5 sts leaving a long tail to seam side.
Fold ears so that purl side fits into knit side. Using long tail left at bind off, seam open side with mattress st. Fold bottom edge together,

enclosing bottom of purl side. Stitch the fold at bottom closed. Attach ears to hat.

Cat Ears (make 2)

Ch co 16.

*Sl 1, p6, k9.

Sl 1, k8, p7*.

Repeat * to * 3 more times.

Sl 1, p2tog, p2, p2tog, k2tog, k4, ssk, k1.

Sl 1, k7, p5.

Sl 1 [p2tog] twice, k2tog, k2, ssk, k1.

Sl 1, k4, p3.

Sl 1, p2tog, k2tog, ssk, k1.

Sc BO 5 sts leaving a long tail to seam side.

Fold ears so that purl side fits into knit side. Using long tail left at bind off, seam open side with mattress st. Attach ears to hat.

Add whiskers by cutting 3 strands of yarn approximately 2 ins. (5 cm) long. Using yarn needle, secure them to face by sewing under one of the duplicate sts in nose area.

Duplicate Stitch

The duplicate stitch is used to embroider a design over the knitted stitches on the fabric.

You will need:

• A tapestry needle

• Yarn in a contrasting color that is the same weight or finer than the one on the knitted fabric.

How to: Insert needle at the bottom of the V through back of work so the needle is at the right side of the knitted fabric. Take the needle to the top right leg of the stitch, pull gently on the working yarn. Insert needle to the left leg of the stitch. Insert needle through the bottom of the V where we began. Take yarn and needle to the next V (insert at the bottom of the V). Repeat with all the other stitches.

Bear face duplicate st chart

15	14	13	12	11	10	9	8	7	6	5	4	3	2	1	
		●			●	●		●	●			●			19
	●	●	●								●	●	●		18
●	●	●	●	●							●	●	●	●	17
●	●	●	●	●							●	●	●	●	16
●	●	●	●	●							●	●	●	●	15
	●	●	●								●	●	●		14
		●										●			13
															12
															11
															10
															9
						●	●	●	●	●					8
						●	●	●	●	●					7
						●	●	●	●	●					6
						●	●	●	●	●					5
							●	●	●						4
								●							3
				●				●		●					2
						●	●	●	●	●					1

Bunny face duplicate st chart

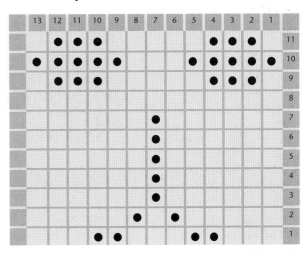

Cat face duplicate st chart

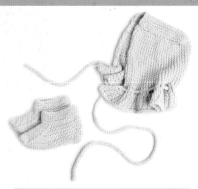

Little Angel

By Kathy Norris

Ruffles and lace for your little angel.

EASY

| Materials |

Knitting Loom

Fine-gauge loom with at least 120 pegs [Sample was knit using Décor Accents fine gauge baby afghan loom]

Yarn

127 yds. (116 m) DK weight yarn [Sample uses Sublime baby cashmere merino silk DK, 75% extra fine merino, 20% silk, 5% cashmere, 1¾ oz (50 g), 127 yds. (116 m) in Piglet 01]

Tools

Knitting tool
Crochet hook
Tapestry needle

Size

6 months

Gauge

22 sts and 30 rows to 4 ins. (10 cm) using single st

Lace pattern for ruffle:
Row 1: K.
Row 2: K1, *yo, ssk; repeat from * ending with k1.

Pattern Notes:
Pattern was designed with cast on from right to left around the loom.

Ruffle
Ch co 120 sts.
Work Lace Pattern for 5 repetitions (total of 10 rows).
K2tog across row, leaving empty pegs between each st to form an eyelet.
K 1 row, forming new loops on empty pegs with e-wrap co.
K 1 row.
K2tog across row, moving sts so that no empty pegs are between pegs with sts.
(60 sts remain for body).

Body
Ss 42 rows.
[Sc BO 24 sts, ss to end of row] twice. (12 sts remain).
Ss 30 rows.
Sc BO all sts.

Finishing
Sew both seams at back using mattress st.
Weave in tails and trim excess.

Bonnet tie
Ch co 4 sts.
K 4-st I-cord for 30 ins. (76 cm).
BO using basic BO method.
Weave in tails and trim excess.

Weave the tie through eyelets at base of ruffle.

Cherub

By Kathy Norris

A quick knit bonnet that will make sure your little cherub is dressed in style!

EASY

St Patterns:
Garter st: *Knit 1 row, purl 1 row, rep * to end.
Stockinette st: Knit every row.

Pattern notes
Pattern was designed with cast on from right to left around the loom.

Body
Ch co 72.
Work garter st for 40 rows.
[Sc BO 28 sts, ss to end of row] twice. (16 sts remain).
Work St st for 40 rows.
Sc BO all sts.

Sew both seams at back using mattress st.
Weave in tails and trim excess.

Bonnet tie:
Ch co 4 pegs.
K 4 st I-cord for 35 ins. (89 cm).
BO using basic bind off method.
Weave in tails and trim excess.

Find center of I-cord and center of back bottom of bonnet. Pin I-cord to bonnet at center. Stretching I-cord, pin to bottom of bonnet on each side of this marked area. This will leave the ends of the I-cord as the ties of bonnet.

Using mattress st, st I-cord tie around bottom of bonnet.
Weave in tails and trim excess.

Materials

Knitting Loom
Fine-gauge loom with at least 120 pegs
[Sample uses Décor Accents fine gauge baby afghan loom]

Yarn

127 yards (116 m) DK weight yarn [Sample uses Sublime baby cashmere merino silk DK, 75% extra fine merino, 20% silk, 5% cashmere, 1¾ oz (50 g), 127 yds. (116 m) in Cuddle 02]

Tools
Knitting tool
Crochet hook
Tapestry needle

Size
6 months

Gauge
26 sts and 40 rows to 4 ins. (10 cm) using stockinette st

Matching Boots for Baby

By Kathy Norris

No need for short rows as this pattern is worked as a flat panel from the bottom of the foot up, with simple shaping to form the toe. One seam later, your boots are finished with ease.

EASY

Materials

Knitting Loom

Fine gauge loom with at least 58 pegs [Sample uses Décor Accents fine gauge baby afghan loom]

Yarn

100 yds. (91.5 m) DK weight yarn [Sample uses Sublime baby cashmere merino silk DK, 75% extra fine merino, 20% silk, 5% cashmere, 1¾ oz (50 g), 127 yds. (116 m) Piglet 01 or Cuddle 02]

Tools

Knitting tool
Crochet hook
Tapestry needle
Stitch markers

Size

6 months

Gauge

26 sts and 40 rows to 4 ins. (10 cm) using stockinette st

Stitch Patterns

Stockinette st = knit every row.

Garter st = * knit 1 row, purl 1 row, repeating from * to end.

Pattern notes

Pattern was designed with cast on from right to left around the loom.

Body (make 2)

Ch co 58.

Work St st for 5 rows. Place st marker on pegs 27 and 32.

Dec row 1: K to 2 sts before peg with marker, k2tog, k6, ssk, k to end of row.

Dec row 2: K to 2 sts before peg with marker, ssk, k6, k2tog, k to end of row.

Repeat dec rows 1 and 2, five more times (34 sts remain).

Repeat dec row 1 once more (32 sts remain).

Work garter st for 10 rows.

Sc BO all sts.

Sew seam at back and sole using mattress st.

Weave in tails and trim excess.

Heirloom Baby Set

By Isela Phelps

Loom knit a baby set that will surely be handed on over generations. Knit with super soft yarn made out of angora and lambswool—perfect for baby-soft items.

INTERMEDIATE

Materials

Knitting Loom

Socks: Fine gauge sock loom with 36 pegs. [Youth (36 peg), fg by Décor Accents was used]
Hat: Fine gauge hat loom with 92 pegs. [Medium (92 peg), fg hat loom by Décor Accents used]

Yarn

150 yds of light worsted weight angora blend [3 skeins of Lorna's Laces Angel, 70% Angora, 30% Lambswool, 50 yds. (46 m) in Green Valley was used in sample]

Tools

Knitting tool
Stitch markers
2 dpn size 2 (2.25 mm)
Stitch holder
Tapestry needle

Size

Socks fit up to size 12 months
Hat: 12 months or 16 ins. (41 cm) head circumference

Gauge

13 sts and 18 rows to 2 ins. (5 cm)

Socks (make 2)
CO 36 sts, join to work in the round.

Rnds 1–16: Work chart rows 1–8 two times.

Begin Heel

* Short-row shaping worked on 18 sts. Place peg markers on pegs 1 and 18.

Row 1: Knit across to peg 17. Wrap peg 18. The last st is now wrapped and remains unworked. Turn.

Row 2: Knit across row to the first peg. Wrap peg 1. This st is now wrapped and remains unworked. Turn.

Row 3: Knit across the row until the peg before the last wrapped peg. Wrap peg. Turn.

Row 4: Knit across to the peg before the last peg wrapped. Wrap peg. Turn.
Repeat Rows 3 and 4, until the 6 middle sts remain unwrapped.

Reverse short-row shaping

(2nd half of heel shape)

Row 1: Work across to the next wrapped peg (peg 13). Knit the loop together with the wrap (treat them as 1 loop). Take the next st off the peg (peg 14) and wrap the peg. This peg now has 2 wraps on it. Turn.

Row 2: Knit across to the next

wrapped peg (peg 6). Knit the loop together with the wrap (treat them as 1 loop). Take the next st off the peg (peg 5) and wrap the peg. This peg now has 2 wraps on it. Turn. Repeat Rows 1 and 2 until you have worked all but the pegs with the st markers (pegs 1 and 18). Pegs 1 and 18 should remain unworked. Yarn will be by peg 2. *

Sock Foot

Worked in the round.

Next round: Start at peg 2 and work around in stockinette st (knit all sts). On pegs 18 and peg 1, be sure to knit the loops and the wraps together (this will eliminate a small hole at each side of the heel). Work 17 rounds in stockinette st (knit all rounds).

Begin Toe

Working a short-row toe is the same as knitting a short-row heel. Work on the first 18 sts and follow the short-row shaping Instructions (from * to *).
Remove sts as follows:
Place on dpn 1 sts from pegs 18–1.
Place on dpn 2 sts from pegs 19–36.
Follow grafting instructions to close the toe (see page 131).

Hat

CO 92 sts, join to work in the round.

Next: Work chart rows 1–8 until item measures 7 ins. (18 cm) from cast-on edge.

Finishing

Take the following sts off and place them on a st holder: 23, 47, 70, and 92.

Bind off the remaining sts in the gather method.

Top Knot

With the remaining 4sts, work a 4-st I-cord, about 5 ins. (12.5 cm) in length. Break yarn and pass the remaining tail through the center of the I-cord to hide tail. Create an overhand knot with I-cord to finish.

Weave in ends and block lightly.

	4	3	2	1		
		●	●			8
		●	●			7
			●	●		6
			●	●		5
	●			●		4
	●			●		3
	●	●				2
	●	●				1

Key

knit knit st

● **purl** purl st

Baby Bunting and Matching Hat

By Denise Layman

Isn't it always the way: the baby falls asleep in his or her warm sleeping bag, then you have to wake them up to put them in the car seat. Not any more. This clever design has a hole to allow the center strap to go right through the bag. We have allowed a hole 10 stitches wide to accommodate a buckle about 8 ins. (20 cm) across. Check your car seat before you begin, as designs may vary.

EASY

Materials

Knitting Loom

Regular gauge knitting loom with at least 60 pegs [Décor Accents baby afghan loom in regular gauge used in sample]

Yarn

350 (400, 515) yds. (320, 365, 470 m) bulky/chunky-weight yarn [Louet Gems Chunky, 100% merino wool, 103 yds. (94 m) per 100 g in Pink Panther used in sample]

Tools

Knitting tool
Tapestry needle

Notions

10 (13) x 1 in. (2.5 cm) buttons

Sizes

Newborn (6–12 months, 12–18 months)

Gauge

8 sts and 12 rows to 2 ins. (5 cm)

Pattern notes
• Baby bunting is knit as two flat panels.
• The smallest size is shown first, followed by larger sizes in brackets. Where only one number appears the instructions apply to all sizes.
• The bunting is worked from the bottom up with the bottom and sides of the piece worked in garter st on the back piece of the bunting, and the buttonband worked as you go with the front of the bunting.
• If another closure such as a zipper or hook and loop closure is desired simply leave out the buttonholes on the front of the bunting.
• Slip the first st of every row.

Dot St Pattern
Row 1: K1, *P1, K3; Rep from * to last 2 sts, P1, K1.
Row 2: K all sts.
Row 3: *K3, P1; Rep from * to last 3 sts, K3.
Row 4: K all sts.

Bottom section of back
Cast on 43 (47, 51) sts with cable cast on method.
All sizes: work 12 rows in garter st

patt ending with a purl row.
Next: Work in St st, cast on 8 sts at the beg of next two rows; 59 (63, 67) sts. The 8 sts at each end of the row will be worked in garter st, in rows 1 and 3 of the dot st patt purl all the edge sts, in rows 2 and 4 knit all the edge sts.

Back body section
Row 1: P8 selvedge sts, k1, *p1, k3; rep from * to last 2 sts of center section, p1, k1, p8 selvedge sts.
Row 2: K all sts.
Row 3: P8 selvedge sts, *k3, p1; Rep from * to last 3 center section sts, k3, p8 selvedge.
Row 4: K all sts.
Work in this patt for 6 (8, 10) ins. (15, 20, 25.5 cm) ending with row 3 of the patt st.
Next Row: K24 (26, 28) sts, BO 10, k to end of row.

Note: It may help to mark the placement of the purl sts in the dot st patt so that the patt may be followed more quickly and easily, especially throughout the shaping of the straps.

Next Row: Follow instructions for dot st patt Row 1, and re-cast on the central sts using an e-wrap co. Cont in patt until the piece is 16 (18, 20) ins. (40.5, 45.5, 50.5 cm) long from first row of the dot st patt.

Next row: BO 7 of the selvedge sts. Work in patt to end of row; 52 (56, 59) sts.

Next row: BO 8 of the selvedge sts. Work in patt to end of row; 44 (48, 52) sts.

Straps

While continuing to follow the dot st patt shape the straps as folls: Work 20 (22, 24) sts in patt, BO 4 center sts, work in patt to end of row. Then work sides separately.

Row 1: Work in patt st to end of row; 20 (22, 24) sts.

Row 2: BO 1 st at each end of the row; 18 (20, 22) sts.

Repeat dec rows while working in the dot st patt until only 10 sts rem. Work even in dot patt for 24 rows.

Next row: Make buttonhole, work 4 sts, BO 2, work to end of row.

Next row: Work all sts in patt casting on the sts BO on the previous row using the e-wrap cast on method.

Switch to St st.

*Next row: K to end of row.

Next row: BO 1 at each end of the row; 8 sts. *

Rep from * to * until 4 sts rem. BO all sts. Repeat strap instructions on the other side of bunting.

FRONT

Cast on 51 (55, 59) sts using the cable cast on method. The last 8 sts on the right end of the piece are the buttonband, these sts are to be worked in the garter st patt, with a buttonhole worked every 12 rows as folls:

Buttonhole

Row 1: K3, BO 2, k3.

Row 2: P3, CO 2 with e-wrap cast on, p3.

Work in this patt for 6 (8, 10) ins. (15, 20, 25.5 cm) ending with row 3 of the dot st patt.

Next Row: K16 (18, 20) sts, then BO the 10 center sts, k to the end of row.

Next Row: Work in patt, casting on the sts that had been BO in the last row using the e-wrap cast on. Cont to knit in patt, working a buttonhole on the buttonband every 12th row, until the piece is 16 (18, 20) ins. (40.5, 45.5, 50.5 cm) from the cast-on edge. BO the first 7 sts of the buttonband sts; 44 (48, 52) sts.

Work strap decreases, as directed for back; however, only work 12 rows when working the 10-st section, and eliminate the buttonhole. BO.

Finishing

Place and secure buttons on side band and straps.

Seam the left side and bottom together overlapping the bottom edge of the buttonband and the side and seaming them together to the bottom edge of the bunting.

Baby Bunting Hat

The hat must be worked on a loom that has a multiple of 4 sts. Typically a newborn hat will be worked on a loom with 36 sts, and a baby hat on a loom with 40 sts. The hat can be made on any loom where the number of pegs are a multiple of 4.

The piece is worked from the base up, starting with the I-cords and earflaps on opposite sides of the loom, and then working in the round for the brim and body.

EARFLAP 1

Cast on and work a 3-st I-cord for 12 ins. (30.5 cm) or desired length. Switch to working a flat piece.

Row 1: K all sts.

Row 2: P all sts.

Row 3: Inc one st at each end of the row for and k to end; 5 sts.

Row 4: P all sts.

Row 5: Inc 1 st at each end of the row, k; 7 sts.

Row 6: P all sts.

Cont to work in garter st for 8 rows ending with a purl row. Break yarn leaving sts on the loom.

EARFLAP 2

Cast on a 3-st I-cord directly opposite the first and repeat procedure for second earflap.

HAT BODY

Cast on all sts on the loom and begin knitting in the round.

Work 9 rows of garter st, switch to dot st patt as folls:

Row 1: K1, *p1, k3*; rep from * to * end of row.

Row 2: K.

Row 3: *K3, p1* repeat from * to * end of row.

Row 4: K.

Work in dot st patt until the hat reaches the desired length, approx. 8–9 ins. (20–22 cm) from cast-on edge of brim.

BO: Remove with gather removal method.

Finishing

Weave in ends, block lightly. Make a pompom, about 2 ins. (5 cm) in diameter, and sew it on the top.

Pinafore Dress

By Isela Phelps

A little dress that is great for all seasons. During the winter, pair the pinafore dress with a lovely white long-sleeved blouse and, during the warm months, wear with a T-shirt. Either way, this item knits fast and provides superb comfort.

EASY

Materials

Knitting Loom

Regular gauge knitting loom with at least 52 pegs [Sample uses baby afghan regular gauge loom by Décor Accents]

Yarn

450 (475, 500) yds. of chunky weight merino wool [Sample uses Louet Gems Chunky, 100% merino wool, 3½ oz (100 g) 103 yds. (94 m) in Crabapple]

Tools

Knitting tool
Tapestry needle
Row counter (optional)
2 buttons ½ in. (1.2 cm) diam

Size(s)

6–12 mos (12–18 mos, 18 mos–24 mos, 4T) [Sample shown in size 4T]
Finished waist measurements: 20 (21, 22, 26) ins. [51, 53, 56, 66 cm]

Gauge

14sts and 22 rows to 4 ins. (10 cm)

Seed Stitch:
Row 1: *K1, p1; rep from * to the end.
Next rows: Repeat row 1.

Back panel
Cast on 40 (44, 46, 52) sts.
Next: Work 6 rows in seed st.

Size 6–12 months
Next: Work 8 rows in St st.
Next: K2, ssk, k to last 4sts, k2tog, k2 (38 sts rem).
Next: Work 6 rows in St st.
Next: K2, ssk, k to last 4sts, k2tog, k2 (36 sts rem).
Next: Work 4 rows in St st.
Next: K2, ssk, k to last 4sts, k2tog, k2 (34sts rem).
Next: Work 4 rows in St st.

Size 12–18 months
Next: Work 8 rows in St st.
Next: K2, ssk, k to last 4sts, k2tog, k2 (42sts rem).
Next: Work 6 rows in St st.
Next: K2, ssk, k to last 4sts, k2tog, k2 (40 sts rem).
Next: Work 6 rows in St st.
Next: K2, ssk, k to last 4 sts, k2tog, k2 (38 sts rem).
Next: Work 6 rows in St st.

Size 2T–3T
Next: Work 10 rows in St st.
Next: K2, ssk, k to last 4sts, k2tog, k2 (44 sts rem).

Next: work 8 rows in St st.
Next: k2, ssk, k to last 4sts, k2tog, k2 (42 sts rem).
Next: work 6 rows in St st.
Next: k2, ssk, k to last 4sts, k2tog, k2 (40 sts rem).
Next: Work 6 rows in St st.

Size 4T
Next: Work 12 rows in St st.
Next: K2, ssk, k to last 4sts, k2tog, k2 (50 sts rem on loom).
Next: Work 10 rows in St st.
Next: K2, ssk, k to last 4sts, k2tog, k2 (48sts rem on loom).
Next: Work 8 rows in St st.
Next: K2, ssk, k to last 4sts, k2tog, k2 (46 sts rem on loom).
Next: Work 8 rows in St st.
Next: K2, ssk, k to last 4sts, k2tog, k2 (44 sts rem on loom).
Next: Work 6 rows in St st.

All sizes
Next: Work 6 rows in seed st.

Front panel
Follow same instructions as for back panel.

Bodice
Next row: BO 4 (4, 4, 6) sts at beg of next 2 rows. (28, 30, 32, 32 sts rem on the loom).
***Next row:** Work the first 4 (4, 4, 6) sts in seed st (maintain the patt from the waistband), knit to the last

4 (4, 4, 6) sts, work the last sts in seed st (maintain the patt from the waistband). *

Repeat from * to * for 18 (20, 22, 22) rows.

Next row: Work first 4 (4, 4, 6) sts in seed st, drop yarn and attach a second skein of yarn. BO 20 (22, 24, 20) sts, work last 4 (4, 4, 6) sts in seed st.

Button Straps

You will work both straps at the same time, each one worked from a different skein of yarn.

Cont working in seed st until each strap measures approximately:
9 (10, 11) ins. [23, 25.5, 28 cm].
Bind off.

Finishing

Block all pieces.

Sew the skirt at both sides with mattress st. Attach a button at the end of each strap. To secure to the back of the skirt, simply pass the button through one of the sts on the back waistline. You have the option of crossing the straps on the back or simply leaving them straight.

Rosette Cardigan

By Denise Layman

This cardigan has a lovely rose motif, just perfect for a little girl.

EASY

Materials

Knitting Loom

Fine gauge loom with minimum of 90 pegs [Décor Accents fine gauge baby afghan loom was used in sample]

 ### Yarn

4 (4, 5 ,6) balls DK in MC

1 ball each DK in CC1 and CC2 [Sample uses Debbie Bliss Baby Cashmerino, 55% merino wool, 33% microfiber, 12% cashmere, 137 yds. (50 g) in 601 Light Pink, 602 Old Rose, 002 Light Green]

Tools

Knitting tool
Tapestry needle

Sizes

6-12 months (12-18 months, 24 months, 3-4T). Sample shown in size 3-4T

Gauge

24 sts and 48 rows to 4 ins. (10 cm)

I-cord edging

Worked over two rows on the last three sts at the edge of the piece:

Row 1: Work to the end of the row where the sts are, knit the 3 I-cord sts.

Row 2: Turn and skip the first 3 sts running the working yarn (wy) behind the pegs, cont to work the row as called for in the patt starting with the st after the I-cord sts. If you are called to purl that first st then bring the wy to the front between pegs 3 and 4, and work the purl st on peg 4. Tug a bit on the I-cord edge sts from time to time to set them, and avoid laddering effect.

Buttonholes

Worked along the buttonband on rows directed in the patt. Number the buttonband sts from left to right as folls: 1 2 3 4.

Work the buttonholes in the center of the garter st buttonband as folls: Move the st from peg 2 to peg 1, move the st from peg 3 to peg 4. Wrap all pegs as normal using the e-wrap to wrap pegs 2 and 3. There will only be one loop on these pegs. It is best to make the buttonhole on a knit row if at all possible.

BACK

Using MC cast on 3 sts and work a 3 st I-cord 94 (100, 106, 112) rows long. Using the I-cord co method cast on 72 (78, 84, 90) sts.

Working as a flat piece knit 12 rows. Knit 6 (3, 6, 3) sts in MC, then begin colorwork chart once making 5 (6, 6, 7) flowers, knit 6 (3, 6, 3) sts in MC. Cont working in this manner through the colorwork chart leaving the selvedge sts in MC.

Knit even in MC, until the piece is 7¼ (8, 8½, 9 ins.) [18, 20.5, 21.5, 23 cm] from the cast-on edge.

Armhole shaping:

BO off 6 sts at the beg of the next two rows. Knit even in MC until the armhole is 4¾ (5, 5½, 5½ ins) [11.5, 12.5, 14, 14 cm] from the beg of armhole.

Shoulder shaping:

BO 9 (11,13, 15) sts at the beg of the next 2 rows.
Work 2 rows even.
BO 4 (7, 8, 10) sts at the beg of the next two rows.
Work two rows even.
BO all remaining sts.

Sleeves (make two)

With MC, cast on three sts and work an I-cord that is 60 (64, 66, 70) rows long.
Using the I-cord cast on method cast on 40 (42 , 44, 48) sts.
Knit 5 rows.
Next row: inc 1 st at each end of the row 42 (44, 46, 50) sts.
* Work 10 rows even.
Next Row: Inc 1 st at each end of the row.*

Repeat from * to* until there are 56 (62, 66, 68) sts on the loom and work even until the sleeve measures 7 (8, 10, 11) ins. [18, 20.5, 25.5, 28 cm].
BO all sts loosely.

Right Front

Note: Buttonholes are worked every 17th (18, 20, 20) row with the first buttonhole worked in row 5.
Cast on 3 sts and make an I-cord 58 (64, 68, 70) rows long.
Do not BO.

Leaving the live I-cord sts on the loom, and using the I-cord cast on; work an I-cord cast on starting with the first peg to the right of the live I-cord Sts. Cast on 36 (42, 46, 48) sts. For a total of 39 (45, 48, 51) sts (this incs the I-cord edge sts).

Note: If there are not enough rows in the I-cord to cast on the number of sts called for simply knit a few more rows of I-cord and add the sts needed shifting the I-cord sts over to make space.
The three I-cord sts will cont to be used for the I-cord edging as described above for the entire length of the piece.
The next 4 sts to the right of the I-cord edging will be worked in garter st (knit one row purl one row). These sts make up the buttonband and will cont until the beg of the neck increases. Begin with a purl row. The remaining sts are worked in knit st.
Work 11 rows establishing the garter st buttonband and I-cord edging at the left edge of the work.

Begin colorwork chart as folls:
Knit 4 (1, 3, 4) sts in MC, then begin with row 1 of colorwork chart, repeat chart (3, 3, 3) times, K 4 (1, 3, 4) sts MC, work the 4

buttonband sts in patt, and edging sts as established.
Cont with the colorwork chart, buttonband, selvedge and edging sts until colorwork is complete.
Work even in MC until the piece is 6½ (7, 7, 8½) ins. [16.5, 18, 18, 21.5 cm] from the cast-on edge.
BO 6 sts at the plain edge for beg of armhole.
Work 12 rows even.

Begin decreasing for neck:

Stop working garter st in the 4 buttonband sts, and simply begin to work knit st.
To dec for the neck opening, * work to 2 sts before the I-cord sts and then K2tog, by moving the loop next to the I-cord sts over one peg to towards the center, shift the I-cord sts over one to close the gap, and knit to the end of the row.
K one row even*.
Repeat from * to* above 17 times or until the armhole reaches 4¾ (5, 5½, 5½) ins. [11.5, 12.5, 14, 14 cm] in length; ending on the right edge of the piece.

Shoulder shaping:

At the beg of the next row, BO 9 (11, 13, 15) sts. Work to the end of the row.
K one row even.
At the beg of the next row BO 4 (7, 8, 10) sts. Work to the end of the row.
K one row even.
Next row, BO all remaining sts, leaving the I-cord sts on the loom.

Work an I-cord that is approx 3 ins. (7.5 cm) long, and place the live sts on a piece of waste yarn for use later. This will be the edging for the sides and back of the neck opening.

Left Front

Cast on 3 sts and make an I-cord 58

(64, 68, 70) rows long.
Do not BO.
Leaving the live I-cord sts on the loom, and using the I-cord cast on work from the live sts to the left of the I-cord sts and cast on 36 (42, 46, 48) sts.
The three I-cord sts will cont to be used for the I-cord edging. The next 4 sts next to the I-cord edging will be worked in garter st (knit one row, purl one row) These make up the buttonband. Begin with a purl row. The remaining sts are worked in knit st.
Work 11 rows establishing the I-cord edging and garter st buttonband and ending on the left end of your work.

Begin colorwork chart as folls:
Knit 4 (1, 3, 4) sts in MC, then begin with row 1 of colorwork chart, repeat chart 2 (3, 3, 3) times, K 4 (1, 3, 4) sts in MC, work the 4 buttonband sts in established patt, and the edging sts as established.
Cont with the colorwork chart, buttonband and selvedge sts until colorwork is complete.

Work even in MC until the piece is 7¼ (8, 8½, 9) ins. [18, 20.5, 21.5, 23 cm] from the cast-on edge.
BO 6 sts at the plain edge for beg of armhole.
Work 12 rows even.

Begin decreasing for neck:

Stop working garter st in the 4 buttonband sts, and simply begin to work knit st.
To dec for the neck opening, * work to 2 sts before the I-cord sts and then K2tog, by moving the loop next to the I-cord sts over one peg towards the center, shift the I-cord sts over one to close the gap, and knit to the end of the row.
K one row even. *

Repeat from * to* above 17 times
or until the armhole reaches 4¾ (5,
5½, 5½) ins. [11.5, 12.5, 14, 14 cm]
in length, ending on the left edge.
At the beg of the next row BO 9
(11, 13, 15) sts. Work to end of row.
K one row even.

At the beg of the next row BO 4
(7, 8, 10) sts. Work to the end of
the row.
K one row even.
Next row BO all remaining sts,
leaving the I-cord sts on the loom.

Work an I-cord approximately 3 ins.
(7.5 cm) long and place the live
sts on a piece of waste yarn for use
later. This will be the edging for the
sides and back of the neck opening.

Finishing
Using an invisible seam join the
fronts and back pieces at the
shoulders. Using mattress st, join
the I-cord neck edging onto the
sides and back of the neck opening,
the ends of the two I-cords should
meet at the center back. The I-cord
may be too long; simply unravel
the I-cords until they are the correct
length to meet and join the two
ends using the live sts.

Center the top edge of the sleeve in
the armhole and join.
Starting at the bottom edge of the
sweater, seam working up the sides
and then cont down the arms.
Place and attach buttons.
Weave in all loose ends.

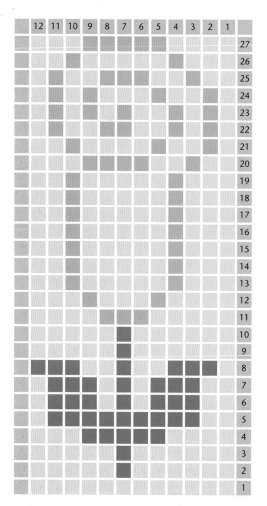

Hearts Cardigan
by Isela Phelps

This chunky-knit cardigan will work up quickly, which is just as well, as all small girls will be clamoring for one.

INTERMEDIATE

Materials

Knitting Loom

Green Knifty Knitter

Yarn
Chunky-weight yarn [Plymouth Encore Chunky 75% acrylic, 25% wool, 143 yds. (131 m) 1 (2) skeins MC, 1 skein CC]

Notions

Knitting loom tool
Crochet hook
Tapestry needle
5 x ½ in. (1.5 cm) diam buttons
Stitch holder

Sizes

3–6 months (12–18 months, 24 months)

Gauge

6 sts and 11 rows to 2 in. (5 cm)

Pattern notes

• The body of the sweater is knitted in the knit st in the main color, the colorwork is added after with duplicate st. This way there are no floats to get tangled and caught up when dressing the child.
• Slip the first st of each row on every piece of the sweater.

Stitch pattern:

1 x 1 rib: K 1, p1.

Back

In main color:
Cast on 30 (32, 36 sts) Work in 1 x 1 rib for 6 rows.
Change to knit st, and knit for 38 (44, 50) rows ending on the left side of the piece.

Neck shaping (working on left side of piece)
Starting at the left edge and working towards the center.

Row 1: Knit 12 (14, 16) sts.
Row 2: Turn and knit 11 (13, 15) sts back to the left side of the piece.
Row 3: Knit 10 (12, 14) sts.
Row 4: Turn and knit 9 (11, 13) sts back to the left edge of the piece.
Row 5: Knit 8 (10, 12) sts. Break yarn leaving a 3 ins. (7.5 cm) tail for weaving in end.

On right side of the piece
Join yarn and work starting from the right edge of the piece and knitting towards the center.
Row 1: Knit 12 (14, 16) sts.

Row 2: Turn and knit 11 (13, 15) sts back to the right side of the piece.
Row 3: Knit 10 (12, 14) sts.
Row 4: Turn and knit 9 (11, 13) sts back to the right edge of the piece.
Row 5: Knit 8 (10, 12) sts. Break yarn leaving a 3 ins. (7.5 cm) tail for weaving in end.

Remove the first 7 (9, 11) live sts on the left side of the piece onto a piece of waste yarn or st holder. Remove the center 10 (12, 14) live sts from the loom and place them on a second piece of waste yarn or st holder. Remove the remaining 7 (9, 11) sts from the right side of the piece and place them on a piece of waste yarn or a st holder. Set aside.

Left front

Cast on 15 (16, 18) sts and work in 1 x 1 rib for 6 rows.
Switch to knit st and knit 38 (44, 50) rows.

Begin neckline shaping

Starting at the left edge of the piece and working towards the center.

Row 1: Knit 12 (14, 16) sts.
Row 2: Turn and knit 11 (13, 15) sts back to the left side of the piece.
Row 3: Knit 10 (12, 14) sts.
Row 4: Turn and knit 9 (11, 13) sts back to the left edge of the piece.
Row 5: knit 8 (10, 12) sts. Break yarn leaving a 3 ins. (7.5 cm) tail for weaving in end.
Remove the first 7 (9, 11) live sts

on the left side of the piece onto a piece of waste yarn or st holder. Remove the remaining sts to a separate piece of waste yarn or st holder.

Right Front
Cast on 15 (16, 18) sts and work in 1 x 1 rib for 6 rows.
Switch to knit st and knit 38 (44, 50) rows.

Begin neckline shaping
Work starting from the right edge of the piece and knitting towards the center.

Row 1: Knit 12 (14, 16) sts
Row 2: Turn and knit 11 (13, 15) sts back to the right side of the piece.
Row 3: Knit 10 (12, 14) sts.
Row 4: Turn and knit 9 (11, 13) sts back to the right edge of the piece.
Row 5: knit 8 (10, 12) sts. Break yarn leaving a 3 ins. (7.5 cm) tail for weaving in end.

Remove the 7 (9, 11) sts from the right side of the piece and place them on a piece of waste yarn or a st holder. Remove the remaining sts to a separate piece of waste yarn or st holder.

Neckband (same all sizes)
Before starting the neckband you must join the fronts and the back at the shoulder. With the right sides of the fronts facing together, line them up at the edges and join using either a three needle BO or the Join Method on the knitting loom. Work from the outside edge of the piece towards the center/neckline. Do not secure the last st. Place it on the waste yarn with the other neckline sts.

To create the neckband, place all 36 sts that are held in reserve back on the loom. Start with the left front, then the seam st, the back sts, the second seam st and the right front sts.
Work in 1 x 1 rib for 6 rows as a flat piece. BO loosely.

Buttonband
To create the buttonband pick up 28 (30, 34) sts along the right front for girls, and the left front for boys.

To pick up the sts put the edge right side facing you inside the loom. Make a slip knot with your working yarn and hold it behind the piece. Using a crochet hook push through the piece in the space between the first and second row at the bottom of the piece where the last row has been created by the slipped sts. Pull the slip knot through and place on the first peg of the loom. Continue to work your way up the piece pulling the working yarn through the piece to create loops on the loom. When the desired number of sts has been cast on; work 6 rows of 1 x 1 rib. BO loosely.

Note: No buttonholes are needed so long as buttons of half an inch (1.5 cm) in size are used.

Sleeves (make two)
Cast on 16 (20, 22) sts. Work in 1 x 1 rib for 6 rows. Switch to the knit st and work for 35 (40, 44) rows increasing one st on both edges of the sleeve every 4 (4, 5) rows ending with at total of 30 (34, 36) sts.
BO loosely leaving an 18 ins. (46 cm) tail for seaming.

Assembly
Lay out the entire body of the sweater with the wrong side facing up. Place the sleeves centered on the body and pin in place. Using the mattress or slip st crochet st, attach the sleeves to the body of the sweater. Then seam the sides and sleeves.
Place buttons on the side opposite the button band and secure. Weave in the ends.

Adding the motif
Using contrast color yarn and the duplicate st, add the color motif of your choice. Sample motifs have been provided in the charts below.

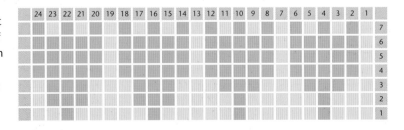

Sailboat Cardigan

By Denise Layman

Any young man would be pleased to wear this little cardigan with its sailboat motif.

EASY

Materials

Knitting Loom

Fine gauge loom with minimum of 91 pegs [Décor Accents fine gauge baby afghan loom was used in sample]

Yarn

[Debbie Bliss Baby Cashmerino, 55% Merino wool, 33% microfiber, 12% cashmere, 137 yds. (125 m) per 50 g was used in sample]
4 (4, 5, 6) balls MC (202 Light Blue), 1 ball each CC1 (700 Red) CC2 (01 Ecru)

Notions

Knitting tool
Tapestry needle
4 buttons
Sewing thread in a matching color
Sharp needle

Sizes

6–12 mos (12–18 mos, 24 mos, 3–4T) Sample shown in size 3–4T

Gauge

24 sts and 48 rows to 4 ins. (10 cm)

Back

Using MC cast on 3 sts and work a 3 st I-cord 94 (100, 106, 112) rows long.
Using the I-cord cast on method cast on 72 (79, 85, 91) sts.
Working as a flat piece knit 12 rows.

Knit 6 (3, 6, 3) sts in MC, then begin colorwork chart once making 5 (6, 6, 7) boats. Knit 6 (3, 6, 3) sts in MC. Cont working in this manner through the chart leaving the selvedge sts in MC.
Knit even in MC, until the piece is 7¼ (8, 8½, 9) ins. [18, 20.5, 21.5, 23 cm] from the cast-on edge.

Armhole shaping:

BO 6 sts at the beg of the next two rows, for beg of armhole.
Knit even in MC until the armhole is 4¾ (5, 5½, 5¾) [12, 13, 14, 14.5 cm] from the beg of armhole.

Shoulder shaping:

BO 9 (11, 13, 15) sts at the beg of the next 2 rows.
Work 2 rows even.
BO 4 (7, 8, 10) at the beg of the next two rows.
Work two rows even.
BO all remaining sts.

Sleeves (make two)

With MC, cast on three sts and work an I-cord that is 60 (64, 66, 70) rows long.
Using the I-cord cast on method cast on 40 (42, 44, 48) sts.

Knit 5 rows.
Next row: Inc 1 st at each end of the row 42 (44, 46, 50) sts.
* Work 10 rows even.
Next row: Inc 1 st at each end of the row. *

Repeat from * to * until there are 56 (62, 66, 68) sts on the loom and work even until the sleeve is 7 (8, 10, 11) ins. [18, 25.5, 28 cm] long. BO all sts loosely.

Right front:

Cast on 3 sts and make an I-cord 58 (64, 68 ,70) rows long.
Do not bind off.

Leaving the live I-cord sts on the loom, and using the I-cord cast on; work an I-cord cast on starting with the first peg to the right of the live I-cord Sts. Cast on 35 (42, 46, 48) sts. For a total of 38 (45, 48, 51) sts (this includes the I-cord edge sts).
Note: If there are not enough rows in the I-cord to cast on the number of sts called for simply knit a few more rows of I-cord and add the sts needed shifting the I-cord sts over to make space.
The three I-cord sts will cont to be used for the I-cord edging as described above for the entire length of the piece.

The next 4 sts to the right of the I-cord edging will be worked in garter st (knit one row, purl one row). These sts make up the buttonband and will cont until the beg of the neck increases. Begin with a purl row. The remaining sts are worked in knit st.

Work 11 rows establishing the garter st buttonband and I-cord edging at the left edge of the work.

Begin colorwork chart as folls:
Knit 10 (2, 4, 5) sts in MC, then begin with row 1 of colorwork chart, repeat chart 1 (2, 2, 2) times, K 10 (2, 4, 5) sts MC, work the 4 buttonband sts in established patt, and edging sts as established. Cont with the colorwork chart, buttonband, selvedge and edging sts until colorwork is complete. Work even in MC until the piece is 7¼ (8, 8½, 9) ins. [18, 20.5, 21.5, 23 cm] from the cast on edge.

BO 6 sts at the plain edge for beg of armhole.
Work 12 rows even.

Begin decreasing for neck
Stop working garter st in the 4 buttonband sts, and simply begin to work knit st.
To dec for the neck opening, *work to 2 sts before the I-cord sts and then K2tog, by moving the loop next to the I-cord sts over one peg to towards the center, shift the I-cord sts over one to close the gap, and knit to the end of the row. K one row even*

Repeat from * to* above 17 times or until the armhole reaches 4¾ (5, 5½, 5¾) ins. [12, 12.5, 14.5 cm] in length, ending on the right edge of the piece.

Shoulder shaping
At the beg of the next row BO 9 (11, 13, 15) sts. Work to the end of the row.
K 1 row.

At the beg of the next row BO 4 (7, 8, 10) sts. Work to the end of row. K 1 row.

Next row: BO all remaining sts, leaving the I-cord sts on the loom. Work an I-cord that is approximately 3 ins. (7.5 cm) long, and place the live sts on a piece of waste yarn for use later. This will be the edging for the sides and back of the neck opening.

Left front:
Note: The 4 buttonholes are worked into this piece in the buttonband as described above. Buttonholes are worked every 17 (18, 20, 20) rows with the first buttonhole worked in row 5.
Cast on 3 sts and make an I-cord 58 (64, 68, 70) rows long. Do not BO. Leaving the live I-cord sts on the loom, and using the I-cord cast on work from the live sts to the left of the I-cord sts and cast on 35 (42, 46, 48) sts.

The three I-cord sts will cont to be used for the I-cord edging. The next 4 sts next to the I-cord edging will be worked in garter st (knit 1 row, purl 1 row). These make up the buttonband. Begin with a purl row. The remaining sts are worked in knit st.

Work 11 rows establishing the I-cord edging and garter st buttonband and ending on the left end of your work.

Begin colorwork chart as folls:
Knit 10 (2, 4, 5) sts in MC, then begin with row 1 of colorwork chart, repeat chart 1(2, 2, 2) times, K 10 (2, 4, 5) in MC work the 4 buttonband sts in established patt, and the 3 I-cord edging sts as established.
Cont with the colorwork chart,

buttonband, selvedge and edging sts until colorwork is complete.

Work even in MC, until the piece is 7¼ (8, 8½, 9) ins. [19, 20, 21.5, 23 cm] from the cast on edge.
BO 6 sts at the plain edge for beg of armhole.
Work 12 rows even.

Begin decreasing for neck
Stop working garter st in the 4 button-band sts, and simply begin to work knit st.
To dec for the neck opening, *work to 2 sts before the I-cord sts and then K2tog, by moving the loop next to the I-cord sts over one peg to towards the center, shift the I-cord sts over one to close the gap, and knit to the end of the row. K one row even. *
Repeat from * to* above 17 times or until the armhole reaches 4¾ (5, 5¼, 5½) ins. [11.5, 12.5, 13, 14.5 cm] in length; ending on the left edge of the piece.

Shoulder shaping
At the beg of the next row, BO 9 (11, 13, 15) sts. Work to the end of the row.
Next row: K.
Next row: BO 4 (7, 8, 10) sts. Work to the end of the row.
Next row: K.
Next row: BO all remaining sts, leaving the I-cord sts on the loom.

Work an I-cord approximately 3 ins. (7.5 cm) long, and place the live sts on a piece of waste yarn or st holder for use later. This will be the edging for the sides and back of the neck opening.

Finishing
Using an invisible seam join the fronts and back pieces at the shoulders. Using mattress st join

the I-cord neck edging onto the sides and back of the neck opening, the ends of the two I-cords should meet at the center back. The I-cord may be too long, simply unravel the I-cord until they are the correct length to meet and join the two ends using the live sts.

Center the top edge of the sleeve in the armhole and join.
Starting at the bottom edge of the sweater, seam working up the sides and then cont down the arms.
Place and attach buttons.
Weave in all loose ends.

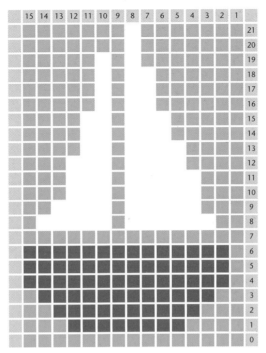

PART II
Big Kids

Sleeveless Ribbed Top

by Bethany Dailey

This stylish top is both classic and trendy. Knitted in a ribbed design using washable fibers, your active girl will wear this with no-worry comfort. The magic of this design comes through the stitch pattern that offers one-size-fits-all ease.

EASY

Materials

Knitting Loom

Knifty Knitter Long Blue Loom (or any large gauge loom with at least 46 pegs)

Yarn

Bulky-weight yarn [sample uses Yarn Art Charme, 230 yds. (212 m), 8 oz (225 g) 45% wool, 42% polyamide, 13% acrylic in 462]

Tools

Knitting tool
J-10 (6 mm) crochet hook
Tapestry needle
Stitch holders
Row counter

Sizes

Girls' sizes 8, 10, 12 yrs: The ribbed style of the garment is such that this style will fit all three sizes. Excellent for growing girls! If a different size is preferred, use the gauge to determine how the number of sts and rows will need to be adjusted for the instructions below.
Finished Chest Measurement: fits up to 30 ins. (76 cm) chest

Gauge

16 sts and 26 rows to 4 ins. (10 cm)

Double rib:

R1: *K2, p2; rep from * to the end. Following rows, knit the knit sts, purl the purled sts.

Front

Cast on 46 sts.
Rows 1–60: Work in double rib st
Rows 61–69: While maintaining the rib st: Dec 2sts at each end. (32 sts rem on loom).
Rows 70–84: Work even in st patt.

Neckline shaping

Rows 85–91: Using only the first 16 pegs, knit in patt, beg at the end, and ending in the middle.
Rows 92–93: Remove middle peg's loop and place onto a crochet hook. Bring your working yarn over the hook, and pull through loop already on hook (Yarn Over: YO, ch 1). Rep until you have 5 empty pegs. The rem loop will be placed back on the next peg in line. Knit in patt to the end of row and back.
Rows 94–97: Rep previous step for neckline BO, but only emptying one peg for every 2 knit rows. You will end up with 9 pegs with loops.
Row 98–100: Rep previous step for neckline BO, emptying only one peg for row 98, leaving you with 8 pegs with loops.
Knit in patt, using these 8 pegs for 3 rows. Place these 8 live sts onto a st holder.
Trim yarn to 5 ins. (12.5 cm). CO to other 16 pegs, put row

counter back to 84, and rep neckline shaping on this side.

Back

Foll instructions as for front until row 68.
Rows 69–90: Work even in st patt.
Row 91: While maintaining st patt: Dec 2sts at each end.
Row 92–94: Work even in patt. Using a st holder, or length of waste yarn, remove the middle 5 loops from their pegs.
Row 95: Dec 1st and work to end in patt.
Rows 96–98: Add one more loop on the side just knitted to the st holder, and knit the row in patt. Repeat 2 more times.
Rows 99–100: Work even in patt. Repeat for the other side from rows 95 to 100.

Finishing

Bringing your front panel up through the inside of the loom, with right sides together, crochet-BO your shoulder seams and back neck edge. Do this by beg at the outside edge and placing the loop from the first peg onto your crochet hook. Then release the first live loop from your front panel st holder and placing it onto your crochet hook, pulling the 2nd through the 1st, and letting it fall off the end of your hook. Alternate adding loops from your loom and your st holder until your first shoulder is completely BO.

Fasten off securely.
BO your back neck edge with basic bind off method.
BO shoulder using the crochet BO method. Sew the sides, leaving a 1½ ins. (4 cm) slit at the bottom of each side open.
Block lightly.

Daisies Skirt

By Isela Phelps

What little girl wouldn't love this cute skirt. The elasticized waist makes it easy to wear, and the daisy embroidery, threaded ribbon, and scalloped edging keep it very pretty.

INTERMEDIATE

Materials

Knitting Loom

Knitting loom with at least 64 pegs in regular gauge [Sample was knit using Décor Accents baby afghan loom]

Yarn

200 (250, 300, 400) yds. (183, 228.5, 274, 366 m) of bulky-weight cotton [sample knit using Blue Sky Alpacas dyed organic cotton, 3½ oz (100 g) 150 yds. (137 m) in Periwinkle]

1 yd. (1 m) of contrasting yarn [Sample uses Blue Sky Alpacas dyed organic cotton, 3½ oz (100 g), 150 yds. (137 m) in Honeydew]

Tools and notions

Knitting tool
Tapestry needle
20 (22, 24, 25) ins. [51, 56, 61, 63.5 cm] of 1½ ins. (4 cm) elastic
3/8 ins. (1 cm) wide grosgrain ribbon 28 (30, 32, 34) ins. [71, 76, 81, 86 cm] long

Sizes

2 (4, 6, 8) years [sample in size 2]

Gauge

16 sts and 19 rows to 4 ins. (10 cm) in St st

Pattern notes

Item is knit flat as front and back and then seamed.

2 x 2 rib stitch

Rnd 1: *K2, p2; rep from * to the end. Rep rnd 1 until item reaches desired length.

Scalloped garter edge

increasing section: CO 2 sts.
*Rnd 1: K.
Rnd 2: P.
Rnd 3: K1, m1, k1 (3sts on loom).
Rnd 4: P.
Rep rnds 3–4, 3 times (6 sts on loom).
Decreasing Section:
Rnd 1: K1, k2tog, k to the end (5sts total on loom).
Rnd 2: P.
Rep rnds 1–2 until 2 sts rem *.
Rep instructions from * to *.

Directions (make 2)
CO 44 (48, 52, 54) sts.
Waist Section
Rnds 1–6: Work Rib St patt.
Rnd 7: P to the end of row.
Rnds 8–13: Work Rib St patt.

Body section
*Rnds 1–7: K to the end of row.
Rnd 8: K2, m1, k to last 2 sts, m1, k2*.
Rep from * to * 3 (4, 4, 6) more times; 52 (58, 62, 66) total sts.
Next row: Work 8 (8, 12, 12) rows in St st.

Next row: *K2, yo, k2tog, Rep from * to the end of row.
Next row: Work 3 rows in St st. Bind off with basic bind off method.

Bottom Edge: Follow Scalloped Garter Edge instructions: 12 (12, 14, 14) times.
Block all pieces prior to assembly.

Assembly

- Use the mattress st to seam along the two sides of the skirt.
- Sew the two ends of the elastic together. Place elastic along the ribbed waist section. Fold the rib section down (along the purl row) and sew the waist section closed.
- Sew the scalloped garter edge to the bottom of the skirt; if needed, secure the edging with safety pins before sewing it to the body of the skirt.
- Pass ribbon through eyelets. Sew the two ends together and leave this seam towards the inside of the skirt.

Once assembled, embroider two lazy daisies to the front of the skirt (see page 135). Sample has two daisies on the left side of the skirt.

22 (24, 26, 27) ins.
[56, 61, 66, 69 cm]

11½ (13½, 14½, 18) ins.
[29, 34, 37, 46 cm]

28 (29, 31, 33) ins.
[71, 74, 79, 84 cm]

Children's Crewneck Sweater

by Isela Phelps

Knitted with a bulky-weight yarn, this top knits fast and it is a great stash-buster. Two versions are provided: Knit the sweater completely in stockinette stitch, or insert the cable motif provided for a more intricate design.

Materials

Knitting Loom

Large gauge knitting loom with at least 42 pegs [Sample uses baby afghan loom in large by Décor Accents]

 Yarn

11 (13, 15, 17) oz [312, 369, 425 482 g] chunky-weight yarn [Sample uses GGH Aspen 50% merino wool, 50% microfiber, 1¾ oz (50 g) 63 yds. (57 m) in 26 Chartreuse]

Tools

Knitting tool
Tapestry needle
Cable needle
Row counter (optional)

Sizes

4 (6, 8, 10) years [sample shown in size 4]
Finished Chest Measurements: 26 (28, 30, 32) ins. [66, 71, 76, 81 cm]

Gauge

10 sts and 14 rows to 4 ins. (10 cm)

INTERMEDIATE

Braid Cable (worked over 8 sts)
Row 1: P1, 4-st LC, k2, p1.
Row 2: P1, k6, p1.
Row 3: P1, k2, 4-st RC, p1.
Repeat Rows 1–3.

Pattern notes

Two versions of the crewneck sweater are provided:
1. Simple version: work the instructions as provided.
2. Cable version: the cable is only worked on the front-left side of sweater (cable will be on the right-hand side of the loom).
Size 4: Place cable on pegs 3–10.
Size 6: Place cable on pegs 4–11.
Size 8: Place cable on pegs 5–12.
Size 10: Place cable on pegs 6–13.
Follow the instructions below and insert the cable on the pegs specified above. Cable is worked to bind-off edge.

Back

* Cast on 34 (36, 40, 42) sts.
Rows 1, 3, 5, 7: * K1, p1; rep from * to the end of row.
Row 2, 4, 6, 8: Knit the knits, purl the purled sts.
Set row counter and keep track of the number of rows knitted.
For Cable Version: insert cable from this point forward on pegs specified.
Next: Work in St st for 26 (28, 30, 34) rows.

Armhole shaping

Next: Bind off 2 (3, 3, 3) sts at beg of next two rows*.
Next: Work 20 (22, 24, 26) rows in St st (or until armhole measures 6½ (7, 7½, 8) ins. [16.5, 18, 19, 20.5 cm]
Next: Bind off all sts

Front

Follow instructions for back from * to *.
Next: Cont working in St st for 12 (14, 16, 18) rows (about 3½, 4, 4½, 5) ins. [9, 10, 11.5, 12.5 cm].

Neckline shaping

Both sides will be worked at the same time. Yarn will be attached to work the 2nd side. Yarn should be on right side.

Size 4:
Next: K12, bind off 6sts. Attach 2nd ball of yarn and work last 12sts.
Size 6:
Next: K12, bind off 7sts. Attach 2nd ball of yarn and work last 12sts.
Size 8:
Next: K14, bind off 6sts. Attach 2nd ball of yarn and work last 14sts.
Size 10:
Next: K14, bind off 8sts. Attach 2nd ball of yarn and work last 14sts.

All sizes:
Next row: Knit to last 2 sts of section (at neck edge), ssk. Drop yarn and pick up yarn for the other section. K2tog, knit to end of row. Repeat above row until, 8 (9, 10, 11) sts rem.

Cont working in established patt until 22 (24, 26, 28) rows have been worked from armhole shaping, until armhole measures 6½ (7, 7½, 8 ins.) [16.5, 18, 19, 20.5 cm].

Sleeves (make 2)
Cast on 18 (18, 19, 20) sts.
Rows 1, 3, 5, 7: * K1, p1; rep from * to the end of row.
Row 2, 4, 6, 8: Knit the knits, purl the purled sts.
Next row: Yo, k1, knit to last st, yo (2 sts inc).

Size 4:
Next: [Work 4 rows in St st.
Next row: yo, k1, knit to last st, yo.] 6 times. 32 sts on loom.

Size 6:
Next: [Work 3 rows in St st.
Next row: Yo, k1, knit to last st, yo.] 3 times.
Next: [Work 4 rows in St st.
Next row: yo, k1, knit to last st, yo] 4 times. 34 sts on the loom.

Size 8:
Next: [Work 3 rows in St st.
Next row: Yo, k1, knit to last st, yo] 2 times.
Next: [Work 4 rows in St st.
Next row: yo, k1, knit to last st, yo] 6 times. 38 sts on the loom.

Size 10:
Next: Work 3 rows in St st.
Next row: yo, k1, knit to last st, yo.
Next: [Work 4 rows in St st
Next row: Yo, k1, knit to last st, yo] 8 times. 38 sts on the loom.

Next: Cont working in St st until St st section measures 10 (11½, 13, 14½) ins. [25.5, 29, 33, 37 cm] (about 36, 40, 46, 52 rows).
Bind off loosely.

Neckband
Cast on 36 sts.
Rows 1, 3: *K1, p1; rep from * to the end of row
Row 2, 4: Knit the knits, purl the purled sts.
Bind off loosely.

Finishing
Block before assembly.
Assemble as follows: Attach sleeves to armholes. Sew sides. Sew on neckband.

Hat and Scarf Set

By Stacey Sobiesiak

Color bursts make this scarf and hat set stand out in a crowd. The simple ribbing and bright colors make this a great last-minute gift for kids and teens.

EASY

Materials

Knitting Loom

60 Peg knitting loom in regular gauge [Sample was knit using regular gauge adult hat loom by Décor Accents]

Yarn

2 skeins each of Bernat Softee Chunky, 100% acrylic, 3½ oz. (100 g) 164 yds. (150 m) in Hot Blue, Hot Lime, True Yellow, Hot Pink and Too Purple

Tools

Knitting tool
Tapestry needle,
Crochet hook
3 large-size knitting needles

Size

Fits child aged 5–8 yrs

Gauge

10 sts and 14 rows to 4 ins. (10 cm)

Pattern notes

Use a double strand of yarn throughout patt.

Hat

Cast on 60 sts with two strands of blue yarn. Join into the round.

Rnds 1–5: *Ss3, p2, repeat from * to end.

Rnd 6: Drop one strand of the blue yarn and join one strand of the green. In established patt work the indicated number of rows in each color:

5 rnds blue/blue
5 rnds blue/green
5 rnds green/green
5 rnds green/yellow
5 rnds yellow/yellow
5 rnds yellow/pink
5 rnds pink/pink
5 rnds pink/purple
5 rnds purple/purple

Finishing

With knitting needles, place 30 sts on each of two needles. Use third needle to work a 3-needle bind off. Create two pompoms and sew one to each corner.

Scarf

Cast on 13 sts with two strands of blue yarn.

Row 1: Ss3, p2, ss3, p2, ss 3. As with the hat, you will drop one strand and replace it with a different color.

In established patt, work the indicated number of rows in each color.

20 rows blue/blue
20 rows blue/green
20 rows green/green
20 rows green/yellow
20 rows yellow/yellow
20 rows yellow/pink
20 rows pink/pink
20 rows pink/purple
20 rows purple/purple

Bind off using a loose binding-off method like the single crochet BO.

PART III
His & Hers

Curly-Q Scarf

By Isela Phelps

This fashionable curlicue scarf will turn heads as well as keep your neck warm.

EASY

Materials

Knitting Loom

12 ins. (30 cm) Regular Gauge or Small Gauge Knitting Board with at least 22 pegs on each side of the board. The pegs must be at least ½–¾ ins. (1.2–2 cm) from center to center.

Yarn

4 MEDIUM — Dk yarn [Sample uses Lamb's Pride in worsted-weight 85% wool, 15% mohair, 190 yds. (174 m) in 145 Spice]

Size

65 ins. (165 cm) length

Pattern Notes

Knit: refers to the flat st throughout the pattern

W&T= Wrap and Turn: Wrap & Turn on a Knit row: Wrap the next peg in a clockwise direction, and cont knitting as pattern.

The pattern is knitted in 2 parts. The 22 pegs will be divided into 2 parts: part 1 has 11 pegs and they will be on one side of the Board. Part 2 has 11 pegs and they will be on the opposite side of the Board.

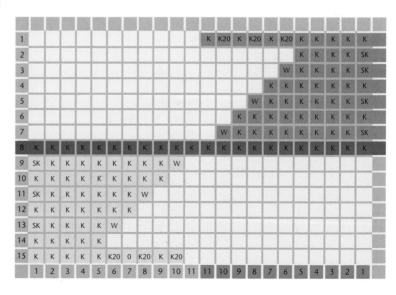

Cast on 11 pegs on side B of the board

11 10 9 8 7 6 5 4 3 2 1

1 2 3 4 5 6 7 8 9 10 11

Cast on 11 pegs on side A of the board

Chart

The following diagram below is a visual of how the pattern is knitted. Each square represents a peg. Each row is a row that you knit. Start reading it at Row 8, from left to right, then you will go from right to left, and then from left to right, up until you reach row 1. Then, move down to row 8, then row 9, row 10 and so on. You will be knitting a flat panel by knitting on both sides of the board.

Definitions for chart:

P = Purl
K = Knit Flat St
SK = Skip the peg
W = Wrap and turn back
K20 = lift 2 over 1, leaving only 1 loop on the peg

Prep Loom: Place markers on pegs 6, 8, 10 on one side of the Board. Place markers on pegs 13, 15, 17 on the other side of the Board. Cast on 11 pegs on one side of the knitting Board. Cross over to the other side and cast on 11 pegs.

Row	1	2	3	4	5	6	7	8	9	10	11	11	10	9	8	7	6	5	4	3	2	1
1												K	K20	K	K20	K	K20	K	K	K	K	K
2																		K	K	K	K	SK
3																	W	K	K	K	K	SK
4																K	K	K	K	K	K	K
5															W	K	K	K	K	K	K	SK
6														K	K	K	K	K	K	K	K	K
7													W	K	K	K	K	K	K	K	K	SK
8	K	K	K	K	K	K	K	K	K	K	K	K	K	K	K	K	K	K	K	K	K	K
9	SK	K	K	K	K	K	K	K	K	W												
10	K	K	K	K	K	K	K	K	K													
11	SK	K	K	K	K	K	K	W														
12	K	K	K	K	K	K	K															
13	SK	K	K	K	K	W																
14	K	K	K	K	K																	
15	K	K	K	K	K	K20	0	K20	K	K20												

Set up row: Knit 11 sts with the flat st on one side of the Board. Knit 11 sts on the other side.

**Row 1: Skip peg 1, K8, W&T peg 10, knit to the end. (Skip 1st peg, 8 pegs are flat stitched, peg 10 has a wrap on it, thus has 2 loops. Turn and knit back to peg 1).

Row 2: Skip peg 1, K6, W&T peg 8, knit to the end.
(Skip 1st peg, knit 6 pegs, peg 8 has a wrap on it, thus has 2 loops).

Row 3: Skip peg 1, K4, W&T peg 6, knit to the end.
(Skip 1st peg, 4 pegs are knitted, peg 6 has a wrap on it, thus has 2 loops).

Check before doing row 4: Pegs 10, 8, and 6 have 2 loops and pegs 1, 2, 3, 4, 5, 7, 9 should have 1.

Row 4: Skip peg 1, K4, [Knit 2 over 1, Knit 1] 3 times.
(Skip 1st peg, knit 4 pegs, Knit 2 over 1 on peg 6, Knit on peg 7,

knit 2 over 1 on peg 8, knit on peg 9, knit 2 over 1 on peg 10, knit on peg 11.)
Cross over to the other side of the Board and knit 11 sts to the end of the row. **
Repeat from ** to ** until you have reached the desired length.

Removal
BO with the flat removal method using a crochet hook.

Materials

Knitting Loom

Yellow Knifty Knitter

Yarn

3½ Skeins of Lamb's Pride Bulky, 85% wool, 15% mohair
1 Skein of Color A
1½ Skeins of Color B
1 Skein of Color C

Tools

Knitting tool
Darning needle
Crochet hook

Size

Pre-felted
Height: 12 ins. (30 cm), depth: 6 ins. (15 cm), wide: 11 ins. (28 cm)

Felted
Height: 9 ins. (23 cm), depth: 4½ ins. (11.5 cm), width: 10 ins. (25.5 cm)

Felted Baguette

By Isela Phelps

An everyday bag completed with a round Knifty Knitter. The felting process mats the yarn, making a stronger and more hardwearing bag.

EASY

Pattern notes

The bag is knitted as a flat panel then it is seamed at the sides and bottom to form the bag.
The bag is knitted in garter st.

Garter St is formed over two rows:
Row 1: Wrap the loom one time with the e-wrap method. Each of the pegs now has 2 loops. Knit over by lifting the bottom loop off the peg.
Row 2: Purl the entire row.

Bag Schematic

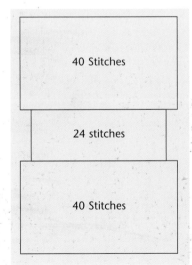

Set up: Using color A: cast on 40 pegs with the Cable Cast-on Method.

Bag Side 1

Working in g st throughout, change colors as follows:

5 Rows with color A.
5 Rows with color B.
2 Rows with color C.
5 Rows with color A.
2 Rows with color B.
4 Rows with color C.
4 Rows with color B.
27 rows of g st (54 rows total).
BO 8 sts on each side of the bag.
(Total 24 sts on the loom).

Bag base

With color B (24 sts).
Knit 16 rows of g st.

Bag side two

Co 8 sts on each side (total 40 sts. and work as folls:
4 Rows with color B
4 Rows with color C
2 Rows with color B
5 Rows with color A
2 Rows with color C
5 Rows with color B
5 Rows with color A
For a Total of 27 rows of g st (54 rows total).
BO completely.

I-cord

Make I-cord with a color of choice.
Step 1: Cast on 3 pegs. Knit 6 rows of I-cord. Leave cord on the loom.
Step 2: Cast on 3 sts (to the right of the pegs used in Step 1) next to the I-cord on Step 1. Knit 6 rows. Cut yarn leaving 5 ins. (12.5 cm) tail.
Step 3: (Combining the 2 I-cords made in steps 1–2 to form one thick

I-cord) With yarn coming from the 3rd peg from I cord on Step 1 go directly to peg 1 on I-cord made in Step 2. Knit a 20 ins. (51 cm) I-cord over the 6 pegs.

Step 4: (Divide the I-cord, into two I-cords as in Steps 1 and 2). With yarn coming from peg 6 go to peg 3 (peg one of I-cord made in Step 1) and knit 6 rows of I-cord on those 3 pegs. BO those 3 pegs. Attach yarn to I-cord still on the loom. Knit 6 rows of I-cord. BO.

Assembly

Seam the sides with the corresponding color of the stripes. If the stripes have color B, then seam that section with color B. If the stripes have color C, then seam it with color C. Seam the bottom of the bag first by following the diagram below. Turn the bag inside out. Seam the sides of the bag to the base of the bag.

Attach the I-cord to the bag

The placement of the I-cord is very important. The I-cord has 2 small I-cords at each end. Make sure that the seam of the bag is between the two I-cords. Place one of the I-cords about ½ in. (1.2 cm) from seam on Side A of the bag. Place the other I-cord about ½ in. (1.2 cm) from seam on Side B. Repeat on the other side of the bag with the opposite end of the I-cord.

Blocking—the finishing touches

Felt for ten minutes in a pillowcase. Stretch your damp bag over a suitable-sized form—in this case a pack of 4 toilet paper rolls. If nothing that resembles the shape is available, use a plastic bag and place plastic bags inside to give it its form. The felted item should fit over the fitted form snuggly. Shape

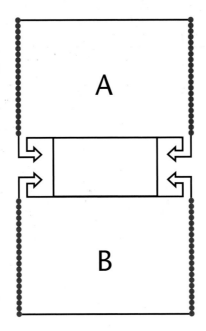

all the corners, and strap; you may have to tug on the strap so it lines up. Make sure that everything looks the way you want it to look. Feel free to pull at it. Do not let it dry until you are completely satisfied with the way it looks. Once it looks the way you desire, let it dry completely **away** from sunlight and from any heating vents. Keep shaping it during the drying process—it may take up to 2 full days to dry completely.

Cascading Shawl

By Stacey Sobiesiak

Wrap yourself in this warm cuddly shawl on cool evenings. This fast and easy pattern works up quickly on a circular loom and easily adapts to different sizes. This project is a great introduction to yarn-over and k2tog.

INTERMEDIATE

Materials

Knitting Loom

A minimum of 59 pegs. Regular Gauge [Sample uses baby afghan loom in regular gauge by Décor Accents]

Yarn

650 yds. (595 m) of Aran-weight wool [Sample was knit using 6 skeins of Noro Silk Garden 45% silk, 45% mohair, 10% wool, 3.5 oz (50g), 110 yds. (100 m) in 84

Tools

Knitting tool
Crochet hook
Blocking wires (to block to rectangle shape)

Sizes

Shawl: Unblocked 22 x 62 ins. (56 x 157 cm)

Scarf: Unblocked 10 x 66 ins. (25.5 x 168 cm).

Sample shown in the first size. Directions for smaller size appear in brackets.

Gauge is not important for this project.

Stitch patterns

Row 1: K1, (k2tog, yo), repeat to last two sts, k2.

Row 2: Knit.

Row 3: K2, (k2tog, yo) repeat to last st, k1.

Row 4: Knit.

*NOTE: On rows 2 and 4 of the pattern, make sure that your loops are loose so you can k2tog on the next rows.

DIRECTIONS

Cast on 59 (27) sts. To make a larger shawl, increase cast on sts in increments of 2.

Row 1: K.

Work in st pattern until desired length

Next: K.

Do not cut yarn. BO with loose BO method. Put first st on a crochet hook, wrap yarn around hook; and pull through first loop. Pick loop off from second peg and pull through the loop already on the crochet hook. Repeat (one loop from peg, one loop made) until all sts are bound off.

Finishing

Weave in ends. Block for a larger shawl or leave in its natural relaxed state.

Tulip Shawl

By Isela Phelps

This cotton yarn lends itself to making a beautiful springtime shawl. Make it as wide as you like. Follow the instructions for a wide shawl, or work two pattern repetitions only and knit as long as desired for a scarf.

INTERMEDIATE

Materials

Knitting Loom

71 peg regular gauge loom [Sample was knit using Décor Accents regular gauge baby afghan loom]

Yarn

4 MEDIUM

14 oz (400 g) of worsted-weight yarn [Sample uses Blue Sky Alpacas Dyed Cotton, 100% organically grown cotton, 3½ oz (100 g) 150 yds. (137 m) in 616 light blue]

Tools

Knitting tool
Peg markers
Blocking wires (to block to rectangle shape)

Size

Sample shown in size 22 x 62 ins. (56 x 157.5 cm)

Gauge

12 sts and 19 rows to 4 ins. (10 cm)

Garter stitch border

Row 1: Knit.
Row 2: Purl.
Rep these 2 rows for 1 g st ridge.

Tulip Pattern (see chart)

Multiple of 10 sts + 3.
Row 1, Row 3: *Yo, central double decrease (cdc), yo, k7*; rep from * to * to last 3sts, yo, cdc, yo.
Row 2 and all even rows: Knit.
Row 5: *K3, yo, ssk, k3, k2tog, yo*; rep from * to* last 3sts, k3.
Row 7: *K4, yo, ssk, k1, k2tog, yo, k1; rep from * to the last 3sts, k3.
Row 9: *K5, yo, cdc, yo, k2; rep from * to the last 3sts, k3.
Row 10: K.
Repeat Rows 1-10.

Pattern notes

Pattern is worked clockwise around loom. First row should be from right to left.

DIRECTIONS

Place a st marker on peg 4 and on peg 68.
Cast on 71sts.

Rows 1–4: Work 4 rows of g st border (2 g st ridges).
Rows 5–14: While maintaining the g st border on the first 4 and last 4 sts, follow the pattern chart in the central 63 sts.

Repeat Rows 5–14: 32 times.
Next row: P to the end.
Next row: K to the end.
Next row: P to the end.
Next row: K to the end.

Finishing

BO with basic BO method.

Block to dimensions above using blocking wires or pins.

Tulip pattern chart

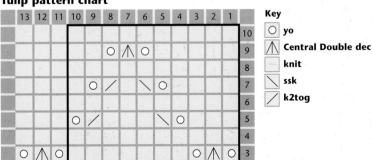

13	12	11	10	9	8	7	6	5	4	3	2	1	

Key
- O yo
- ⋀ Central Double dec
- − knit
- ╲ ssk
- ╱ k2tog

Summertime Top

By Isela Phelps

Loomers know that summertime doesn't mean it is time to put away the looms. This summer, beat the heat by knitting a fun short sleeve top with cooling bamboo ribbon yarn.

INTERMEDIATE

Materials

Knitting Loom

62 (70, 78, 86) peg regular gauge loom.
[Sample uses Décor Accents, baby afghan loom in regular gauge]

Yarn

12 (14, 15, 18) oz [340, 397, 425, 510 g] of heavy worsted ribbon yarn
[Sample uses Tahki Bali, 100% Bamboo, 1¾ oz (50 g) 81 yds. (74 m) in Periwinkle]

Tools

Knitting tool
Tapestry needle
Safety pin to attach bow to the front (optional)
Row counter (optional but extremely helpful)

Size(s)

Small (medium, large, extra-large) [sample shown in small size] Finished measurements
Chest: 32 (36, 40, 44 ins.) [81, 91, 102, 112 cm]
Length: 21 (21, 23, 23 ins.) [53, 58, 58 cm]

Gauge

15sts and 19 rows to 4 ins. (10 cm) in St st

Garter st border
Row 1: Knit.
Row 2: Purl.
Repeat rows 1 and 2 to create garter st (g st) pattern (1 g st ridge).

Stockinette stitch (St st)
Knit all rows.

Back
Cast on 62 (70, 78, 86) sts.
Work in g st for 8 (8, 10, 10) rows. (Start row counter)
Work in St st for 56 (60, 64, 68) rows.
Armhole shaping
Row 1: BO 4 (4, 5, 5) sts at beg of next two rows.
Row 2: Work in St st until you have 96 (102, 108, 110) St st rows.
Shoulder shaping
BO 11 (14, 16, 19) sts at beg of next 2 rows.

Front
Work as for back until armhole shaping row 1.
Cont working in St st for another 26 (26, 28, 28) rows.
Neckline shaping: you will be working both sides at the same time.
Small size:
K 17, join another ball of yarn and cont with this ball of yarn to the next instructions, BO 20, k17.

Medium size:
K 21, join another ball of yarn and cont with this ball of yarn to the next instructions, BO 20, k21.
Large size:
K 23, join another ball of yarn and cont with this ball of yarn to the next instructions, BO 22, k23.
X-large-size:
K 26, join another ball of yarn and cont with this ball of yarn to the next instructions, BO 24, k26.
All sizes:
Work both sides at the same time (one side with one ball of yarn and the other with the other ball of yarn).

Dec 1 st at neck edge every row 6 (7, 7, 7) times. 11 sts (14, 16, 19) sts remains.
Work even until armhole depth measures same as for back (you should have the same number of rows as you did for back).
BO 11 (14, 16, 19) sts.

Sleeves (make 2)
Cast on 38 (41, 44, 47) sts.
Work in g st border for 8 (8, 10, 10) rows. (Start row counter) Change to St st.
Next: Increase 1 st at each end of row on the next 6 (6, 7, 7) rows.
Next: *Work 1 row even.
Next: Increase 1 st at each end of row*.
Repeat from * to * 6 times. 62 (65,

70, 73) sts total on loom.

Next: Work even until you have worked 24 (24, 26, 26) St st rows. BO loosely.

Neckline I-cord

Cast on 4 sts. Work a 4-st, I-cord until you have enough length to go around the neckline.

Bow

Cast on 6 sts. Work in g st border for 16 rows.

To make the center bow gatherer, cast on 3 sts. Work in g st border for 6 rows.

Center bow gatherer on top of the Bow. Sew the bow gatherer close and secure to the bow. Secure it with a safety pin.

Finishing

Block all the pieces. Sew the shoulders first. Then attach the sleeves. Sew the sides of top. Lastly, sew the I-cord to the neckline: be sure to have the two ends of I-cord join at the back of neckline.

A Touch of Lace

By Kathy Norris

This ladies' short sleeve pullover is a delightful knit. With just a touch of lace around the edge, it's perfect for the office or an evening out.

INTERMEDIATE

Lace edging pattern
Row 1: *Ssk, ss3, yo, k1, yo, ss3, k2tog; rep from * to end of row.
Row 2 and all even rows: K 1.
Row 3: *Ssk, ss2, yo, k1, yo, ssk, yo, ss2, k2tog; rep from * to end.
Row 5: *Ssk, ss1, yo, k1, [yo, ssk] twice, yo, ss1, k2tog; rep from * to end of row.
Row 7: *Ssk, yo, k1, [yo, ssk] 3 times, yo, k2tog; rep from * to end.

Pattern notes
• Pattern was designed with cast on from right to left around the loom.
• When patterns says "dec 1":
— ssk if working yarn is on the right side of the loom
— k2tog if working yarn is on the left side of the loom
• Work loosely so that sts can be moved around more easily.
• St st = knit every row

Back
Ch co 99 (110, 121, 132).
P 1 row.
Work lace edging rows ending with an even row.
[*K1, p1, k7, p1, k1; repeat from * to end of row] for 11 rows.
Work St st until back measures 11½ ins. (12, 12½, 13 ins.) [29, 30, 32, 33 cm] from cast on row.

Armhole shaping
Sc BO 5 (6, 6, 7) sts at beg of next 2 rows.
*dec 1, k until 2 sts remain, dec 1.

K 1 row.*
Repeat * to * 6 (9, 11, 14) more times. 75 (78, 85, 88) sts.
Work St st until armhole measures 8 (8½, 9, 9 ins.) [20.5, 21.5, 23, 23 cm].

Shoulder shaping (work for appropriate size)
Small (medium): Sc BO 10 sts at beg of next 2 rows.
Sc BO 11 sts at beg of next 2 rows.
Sc BO rem 33 (36) sts.

Large: Sc BO 7 sts at beg of next 2 rows.
Sc BO 8 sts at beg of next 4 rows.
Sc BO rem 39 sts.

X-large: Sc BO 8 sts at the beg of next 6 rows.
Sc BO rem 40 sts.

Front
Work same as back to armhole shaping.
Armhole shaping
Sc BO 5 (6, 6, 7) sts at beg of next 2 rows.
Dec 1, k until 2 sts remain, dec 1. K 1 row.
Repeat * to * 6 (9, 11, 14) more times. 75 ins. (78, 85, 88) sts.
Work St st until armhole measures 5 (5, 5½, 5½ ins.) [12.5, 14, 14 cm].

Materials

Knitting Loom
Fine gauge loom [Décor Accents fine gauge baby afghan loom used in sample]

Yarn
960 (1090, 1167, 1200) yds. DK yarn [Sample uses Debbie Bliss Cathay, 50% cotton, 35% viscose microfiber, 15% silk, 1¾ oz (50 g), 109 yds. (100 m) in yellow 21]

Tools
Knitting tool
Crochet hook
Tapestry needle

Size(s)
Small 32–34 ins. (medium 36–38 ins., large 40–42 ins., x-large 44 ins.) [81–86 cm, 91–97 cm, 102–107 cm, 112 cm]

Gauge
21.5 sts and 40 rows to 4 ins. (10 cm) using St st, washed and blocked

Shape neck

K 29 (30, 33, 34) sts, sc BO next 17 (18, 19, 20) sts, k 29 (30, 33, 34) sts.

Working each side of neck at the same time (with a separate strand of yarn), dec 1 st at neck edge (k2tog on right neck edge and ssk on left neck edge) for next 8 (9, 10, 10) rows. 21 (21, 23, 24) sts rem for each side.

Working each side of neck at the same time, work St st until armhole measures 8 (8½, 9, 9 ins.) [20.5, 21.5, 23, 23 cm]. Work one side an extra row so that both sides finish with working yarn at armhole edge (not neckline edge).

Shoulder shaping

Work for appropriate size:

Small (medium): Sc BO 10 sts, k rem sts in row.
K 1 row.
Sc BO rem 11 sts.

Large: Sc BO 7 sts, k rem sts in row.
K 1 row.
Sc BO 8 sts, k rem sts in row.
K 1 row.
Sc BO rem 8 sts.

X-large: Sc BO 8 sts, k rem sts in row.
K 1 row.
Sc BO 8 sts, k rem sts in row.
K 1 row.
Sc BO rem 8 sts.

Sleeves (make 2)

Ch co 66 (66, 77, 77).
P 1 row. Work lace edging rows ending with an even row.

Work sleeves for appropriate size:

Small:
[*k1, p1, k7, p1, k1; repeat from * to end of row] for 11 rows.
Work St st for 5 rows.
K1, mk1, k until 1 st rem, mk1, k1.
Work St st for 16 rows.
K1, mk1, k until 1 st rem, mk1, k1
70 sts.

Medium:
[*K1, p1, k7, p1, k1; repeat from * to end of row] for 7 rows.
K1, mk1, *p1, k7, p1, k1, rep from * until 1 st rem, mk1, k1.
[*K2, p1, k7, p1, k2; repeat from * to end of row] for 3 rows.
Work St st for 5 rows.
K1, mk1, k until 1 st rem, mk1, k1.
*Work St st for 8 rows.
K1, mk1, k until 1 st rem, mk1, k1*.
Repeat * to * twice more. 76 sts.

Large:
[*K1, p1, k7, p1, k1; repeat from * to end of row] for 11 rows.
Work St st for 5 rows.
K1, mk1, k until 1 st rem, mk1, k1.
Work St st for 17 rows.
K1, mk1, k until 1 st rem, mk1, k1.
81 sts.

X-large:
[*K1, p1, k7, p1, k1; repeat from * to end of row] for 11 rows.
K 1 row.
K1, mk1, k until 1 st rem, mk1, k1.
*Work St st for 12 rows.
K1, mk1, k until 1 st rem, mk1, k1*.
Repeat * to * once more. 83 sts.

All sizes:
K 1 row.
Sc BO 5 (6, 6, 7) sts beg of next 2 rows.
Dec row 1: K 1 row.
Dec row 2: Dec 1, k until 2 sts remain, dec 1*.
Repeat these 2 dec rows 3 (4, 5, 4) more times.

Dec row 3: K 2 rows.
Dec row 4: Dec 1, k until 2 sts rem, dec 1*.
Repeat these 2 dec rows 11 (11, 11, 13) more times.

Repeat dec rows 1–2, 4 (4, 5, 4) more times.
Sc BO rem 20 (22, 23, 23) sts.

Collar:

Ch co 99 (110, 110, 110) sts.
P 1 row.
Work lace edging rows ending with an even row.
[*K1, p1, k7, p1, k1; repeat from * to end of row] for 11 rows.
Sc BO loosely.

Finishing

Wash and block all pattern pieces. Using mattress st, sew seams together in the following order:

• Sew shoulder seams together
• Sew sleeve cap (top) to armhole(s), easing to fit.
• Sew sleeve seams and body side seams.
• Find center of collar and center back of neckline on sweater. With right side of collar to wrong side of sweater, pin together at center back. Place ends of collar at center of front neckline on sweater and pin. Pin rem area of collar to neckline, easing as necessary. Use mattress st to seam together.
• Weave in tails and trim excess.

Spice

By Kathy Norris

Take a cable stitch and mix it up. Add double seed stitch to the middle. And the result is Spice—a pull-over hoodie that he will want to wear!

INTERMEDIATE

Materials

Knitting Loom

130 peg small gauge knitting loom [Sample was knit using Décor Accents small gauge baby afghan loom]

Yarn

1744 (1853, 1962) yds. [1595, 1695, 1794 m] worsted-weight yarn [Sample uses GGH Tara, 72% cotton, 28% nylon, 1¾ oz (50 g) 109 yds. (100 m) blue 06]

Tools

Knitting tool
Cable needle
Crochet hook
Stitch markers

Sizes

Small 34–36 ins. (medium 38–40 ins., large 42–44 ins.)
Sample shown in size small

Finished Measurements

Chest 38 (43, 47 ins) [97, 109, 119 cm]
Sleeve length 18½ (19, 19½ ins.) [47, 48, 50 cm]

Gauge

17 sts and 25 rows to 4 ins. (10 cm)

Cable Twist: 4-st LC:
Slip 2 sts; k next 2 sts and place on cable needle; bring wy between pegs and cable needle to knit the 2 slipped sts; remove these 2 sts from pegs and place on the 2 empty pegs next to them without twisting.

Double seed St (dss)
Row 1: K2, p2, k2, p2, k2, p2.
Row 2: P2, k2, p2, k2, p2, k2.

Pattern notes
• Co from right to left.
• Front is knitted with 3 cables on each side of the center with dss in between. Once the neck is shaped, the dss and one cable on each side of the dss will no longer be worked.

Back
Chain co 84 (92, 100).
Ribbing row 1: K2, p2; rep from * to end of row.
Ribbing row 2: P2, k2; rep from * to end of row.
Rep ribbing rows 1 and 2, for 1½ ins. (4 cm).
Work St st until back measures 14 ins. (14½ ins., 15 ins.) [36, 37, 38] from co row, ending with wy on the left side of the loom.

Armhole shaping:
Sc BO 4 (5, 5) sts at the beg of the next 2 rows.
*Knit 1 row.
K2tog, knit until 2 sts rem in row, ssk.*
Rep * to * 1 (2, 4) more times with

72, (76, 80) sts rem.
Work St st until armhole measures 8½ (9½, 9¾ ins.) [21.5, 23, 24 cm].

Shoulder shaping (work for appropriate size):
Small: Sc BO 7 sts at the beg of next 2 rows.
Sc BO 8 sts at beg of next 4 rows.
Sc BO rem 26 sts.
Medium: Sc BO 8 sts at the beg of next 6 rows.
Sc BO rem 28 sts.
Large: Sc BO 8 sts at the beg of next 4 rows.
Sc BO 9 sts at beg of next 2 rows.
Sc BO rem 28 sts.

Front
Chain co 84 (92, 100).
Ribbing row 1: K2, p2; rep from * to end of row.
Ribbing row 2: P2, k2; rep from * to end of row.
Rep ribbing rows 1 and 2 for 1 ½ in. (4 cm) ribbing, ending with wy on left side of knitting loom. Place st marker on pegs 12 and 73 (16 and 77; 20 and 81).
Row 1: K to peg with st marker, p2, [k4, p4] twice, k4, p2, dss row 1, p2, [k4, p4] twice, k4, p2, k to end of row.
Row 2: K to peg with st marker, p2, [k4, p4] twice, k4, p2, dss row 2, [k4, p4] twice, k4, p2, k to end of row.
Row 3: Rep row 2.
Row 4: Rep row 1.
Row 5: K to peg with st marker,

p2, 4-st LC, p4, k4, p4, 4-st LC, p2, dss row 1, p2 4-st LC, p4, k4, p4, 4-st LC, p2, k to end of row.

Row 6–7: Rep row 2.

Row 8–9: Rep row 1.

Row 10: Rep row 2.

Row 11: K to peg with st marker, p2, 4-st LC, p4, k4, p4, 4-st LC, p2, dss row 2, p2, 4-st LC, p4, k4, p4, 4-st LC, p2, k to end of row.

Row 12–13: Rep row 1.

Row 14: Rep row 2.

Row 15: K to peg with st marker, p2, k4, p4, 4-st LC, p4, k4, p2, dss row 2, p2, k4, p4, 4-st LC, p4, k4,

p2, k to end of row.

Row 16–17: Rep row 1.

Row 18–19: Rep row 2.

Row 20: Rep row 1.

Row 21: K to peg with st marker, p2, k4, p4, 4-st LC, p4, k4, p2, dss row 1, p2, k4, p4, 4-st LC, p4, k4, p2, k to end of row.

Rep rows 2 to 21 until front is 14 (14½, 15 ins.) [36, 37, 38 cm] from co row, ending after working an even numbered row so that wy is at the left side of the loom.

Armhole shaping

When decreasing to shape armholes, you will decrease at edges and at the same time work the next row of "rep rows" to stay in patt.

Sc BO 4 (5, 5) sts at the beg of the next 2 rows.

*Knit 1 row.

K2tog, work next row of rows 2 to 21 until 2 sts rem in row, ssk.*

Rep * to * 1 (2, 4) more times. 72, (76, 80) sts rem.

Cont working in patt (next row of rows 2–21) until armholes measure 6 (6¼, 6½ ins.) [15, 15.5, 16.5 cm].

Shape neck

Note: The BO and dec of sts to shape the neckline will eliminate dss patt (dss rows 1 and 2) as well as some of the sts used for the cable on both sides of the dss sts. You will need to cont working patt rows 2 to 21 but will not work dss rows or the two cables on either side of the dss sts (these will be knitted or purled as stated in the row instructions instead of the 4-st LC preceding and foll the dss row instructions).

Work first 29 (31, 32) sts of patt row, sc BO next 14 (14, 16) sts, work rem 29 (31, 32) sts of patt row.

Working each side of neck at the same time (with a separate strand of yarn) cont to stay in patt working next row of rows 2–21:

Dec 1 st at neck edge (k2tog on right neck edge and ssk on left neck edge) for next 6 (7, 7) rows. 23 (25, 25) sts rem on each side.

Cont working in patt (next row of rows 2–21) on both sides until armholes measure 8½ (9¼, 9½ ins.) [21.5, 23, 24 cm]. Work one side an extra row so that both sides finish with wy at armhole edge (not neckline edge).

Shoulder shaping (work for appropriate size):
Small: Sc BO 7 sts, work in patt to end of row.
Work next row of patt.
Sc BO 8 sts, work in patt to end.
Sc BO rem 8 sts.

Medium and large: Sc BO 8 sts, work in patt to end of row. Work next row of patt.
Sc BO 8 sts, work in patt to end.
Sc BO rem 9 sts.
Sleeves (make 2)
Ch co 40 (44, 48).
Ribbing row 1: K2, p2; rep from * to end of row.
Ribbing row 2: P2, k2; rep from * to end of row.
Rep ribbing rows 1 and 2 for 1½ ins. (4 cm) ribbing.
*Work St st for 9 rows.
K1, mk1, knit until 1 st left, mk1, k1*.
Rep * to * 8 (10, 10) more times. (58, 66, 70 sts).

Work St st until sleeve measures 18 (18, 18½ ins.) [46, 46, 47 cm] from co row, ending with wy on left side of loom.
Sc BO 4 (5, 5) sts at beg of next 2 rows.

Work sleeves for appropriate size:
Small: *K1 row.
Ssk, knit until 2 sts rem, k2tog*.
Rep * to * 16 more times.
Sc BO rem 16 sts.
Medium: K2tog, knit until 2 sts rem, ssk.
*K1 row.
Ssk, knit until 2 sts rem, k2tog*.
Rep * to * 16 times.
k2tog, knit until 2 sts rem, ssk.

Sc BO rem 18 sts.
Large: K2tog, knit until 2 sts rem, ssk.
*K1 row.
Ssk, knit until 2 sts rem, k2tog*.
Rep * to * 17 times.
K2tog, knit until 2 sts rem, ssk.
Sc BO rem 20 sts.

Tie
Ch co 3 sts.
Knit 3 st I-cord for 50 ins. (127 cm).
BO using basic BO method.
Weave in tails and trim excess, then set aside.

Front band
E-wrap CO 122 (125, 129) sts.
Work St st for 2 rows.
K2, k2tog, knit until 4 sts left, k2tog, k2 (k2tog creates eyelet holes for tie to go through).
Knit next row casting on new sts onto empty pegs.
Work St st for 16 rows.
Lay I-cord tie along knitting inside of loom. Thread ends of I-cord through the eyelet holes. Fold knitting by bringing co row up and placing loops on corresponding peg (as with making a folded brim for a hat), encasing hood tie in the fold.
Knit bottom loop over top loop.

Hood
Work St st for 8 rows (wy is on the right side of loom).
Work hood for appropriate size:
Small:
*K2tog, knit until 2 sts are left, ssk.
Knit 1 row*.
Rep 14 more times with 92 sts rem.
Medium/large:
K2tog, knit until 2 sts are left, ssk.
*Ssk, knit until 2 sts are left, k2tog.

Knit 1 row*.
Rep 14 more times with 95 (97) sts rem.

All sizes:
Work St st until hood measures 7½ ins. (19 cm) not including front band.
Sc BO 35 sts, knit to end.
Rep last instruction once more.
22 (25, 27) sts rem.
Work St st until this section measure 8½ ins. (21.5 cm).
Sc BO rem sts.

Finishing
Block all pieces, and using mattress st sew together in this order:
• Sew shoulder seams together
• Sew sleeve cap (top) to armhole(s), easing to fit.
• Sew sleeve seams and body side seams.
• Sew back seams of hood.
• Locate center of hood back and center of body back at neckline. Using this as guideline, pin hood along back and front of neckline with hood bands at center of front neckline. Sew together.
• Weave in tails and trim excess.

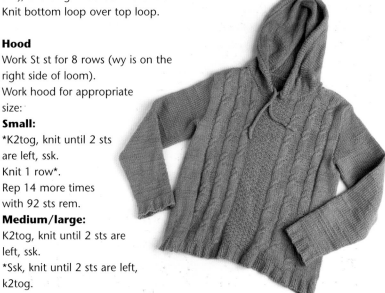

Sugar

By Kathy Norris

This hooded pullover for her uses single stitch for an all-over texture. Since single stitch is a quick knit, you'll find that this pattern really is as sweet as sugar!

INTERMEDIATE

Materials

Knitting Loom

130 peg small gauge knitting loom [Sample uses DA small gauge baby afghan loom]

Yarn

1417 (1526, 1635, 1744) yds. [1296, 1385, 1595 m] worsted-weight yarn [Sample uses GGH Tara, 72% cotton, 28% nylon, 1¾ oz (50 g) 109 yds. (100 m) in peach]

Tools

Knitting tool
Crochet hook

Sizes

Small 32–34 ins. chest (medium 36–38, large 40–42, X-large 44 ins.) [81–86, 91–97, 102–107, 112 cm]. Sample shown in medium

Finished Measurements

Chest 36 (40½, 44, 46 ins.) [91, 103, 112, 117 cm]
Sleeve length 16½ (17, 18, 20 ins) [42, 43, 45, 50 cm]

Gauge

13 sts and 18½ rows to 4 ins. (10 cm) using single st

Pattern notes

Patt was designed with co from right to left around the loom.
When patts says dec 1 ins. (2.5 cm)
- Ssk if wy is on the right side of the loom.
- k2tog if wy is on the left side of the loom.

Back

Ch co 64 (72, 76, 80) sts.
Row 1: *P 1 row.
Row 2: Ss 1 row*.
Rep * to * 4 more times.
P 1 row.
Ss 10 (11, 11, 12) rows.
Dec 1, ss until 2 sts rem, dec 1.
*Ss 4 (3, 6, 4) rows.
Dec 1, ss until 2 sts rem, dec 1*.
Rep * to * 4 (5, 3, 4) more times.
52 (58, 66, 68) sts.
Ss 5 (6, 3, 5) rows.
Ss 1, mk1, ss until 1 st rem, mk1 ss 1.
*Ss 7 (4, 8, 6) rows.
Ss 1, mk1, ss until 1 st rem, mk1 ss 1*.
Rep * to * 2 (3, 2, 3) more times.
60 (68, 74, 78) sts.
Ss 8 (10, 10, 10) rows.

Armhole shaping:

Sc BO 3 (3, 4, 4) sts at beg of next 2 rows.
*Dec 1, ss until 2 sts rem, dec 1.
Ss 1 row*.
Rep * to * 3 (6, 6, 7) more times.
46 (48, 52, 54) sts.

Ss until armholes measure 8 (8½, 9, 9) ins. [20.5, 21.5, 23, 23 cm].

Shoulder shaping (work for appropriate size):
Small (medium): Sc BO 7 sts at beg of next 4 rows.
Sc BO rem 18 (20) sts.
Large: Sc BO 7 sts at beg of next 2 rows.
Sc BO 8 sts at beg of next 2 rows.
Sc BO rem 22 sts.
X-large: Sc BO 8 sts at the beg of next 4 rows.
Sc BO rem 22 sts.

Front

Work same as back to armhole shaping.
Armhole shaping:
Sc BO 3 (3, 4, 4) sts at beg of next 2 rows.
*Dec 1, ss until 2 sts rem, dec 1.
Ss 1 row*.
Rep * to * 3 (6, 6, 7) more times.
46 (48, 52, 54) sts.
Ss until armholes measure 5½ (6, 6, 6) ins. [14, 15, 15, 15 cm].

Shape neck:
Ss 19 (19, 21, 22) sts, sc BO next 8 (10, 10, 10) sts, ss 19 (19, 21, 22) sts.
Working each side of neck at the same time (with a separate strand of yarn) and using single st:
- Dec 1 st at neck edge (k2tog on right edge and ssk on left edge) for next 5 (5, 6, 6) rows.

14 (14, 15, 16) sts on each side. Ss until armholes measure 8 (8½, 9, 9) ins. [20, 21.5, 22.5, 22.5 cm]. Work one side an extra row so that both sides finish with wy at armhole edge (not neckline edge).

Shoulder shaping (work for appropriate size):
Small and Medium: *Sc BO 7 sts, ss to end of row.
Ss 1 row*.
Rep * to * once more.
Sc BO rem 7 sts.
Large: Sc BO 7 sts, ss to end.
Ss 1 row.
Sc BO rem 8 sts.
X-large: Sc BO 8 sts, ss to end.
Ss 1 row.
Sc BO rem 8 sts.

Sleeves (make 2)
Ch co 44 (48, 50, 52).
Ribbing
*P 1 row.
Ss 1 row*.
Rep * to * 4 more times.
P 1 row.
Ss until sleeve measures 16½ (17, 18, 20 ins) [42, 43, 45, 50 cm] from co row, ending with wy on left side of loom.
Sc BO 3 (3, 4, 4) sts at beg of next 2 rows.
38 (42, 42, 44) sts.
Work sleeves for appropriate size:
Small: *Ss1 row.
Ssk, knit until 2 sts rem, k2tog*.
Rep * to * 12 more times.
Sc BO rem 12 sts.
Medium: K2tog, knit until 2 sts rem, ssk*.
*Ss1 row.
k2tog, knit until 2 sts rem, ssk*.
Rep * to * 12 more times.
Sc BO rem 14 sts.
Large: *Ss1 row.
Ssk, knit until 2 sts rem, k2tog*.
Rep * to * 13 more times.
Sc BO rem 14 sts.

X-large: K2tog, knit until 2 sts rem, ssk*.
*Ss1 row.
K2tog, knit until 2 sts rem, ssk*.
Rep * to * 12 more times.
Ssk, knit until 2 sts rem, k2tog.
Sc BO rem 14 sts.

Tie
Ch co 3 sts.
Knit 3 st I-cord for 50 ins. (127 cm)
BO using basic BO method.
Weave in tails and trim excess, then set aside.

Front band
E-wrap co 88 (90, 92, 92) sts.
P 1 row.
Ss 2, k2tog, ss until 4 sts rem, k2tog, ss2 (k2tog creates eyelet holes for tie to go through), P1 row.
Co new sts on empty pegs.
*Ss 1 row.
P 1 row*.
Rep * to * 5 more times.
Ss 1 row.
Lay I-cord tie along knitting inside of loom. Thread ends of I-cord through the eyelet holes. Fold knitting by bringing co row up and placing loops on corresponding peg (as with making a folded brim for a hat), encasing hood tie in the fold.
Knit bottom loop over top loop.

Hood
Ss 5 (6, 6, 6) rows.
Dec 1, ss until 2 sts rem, dec 1.
*Ss 1 row.
Dec 1, ss until 2 sts rem, dec 1*.
Rep * to * 9 (9, 10, 10) more times.

66 (68, 68, 68) sts rem.
Work ss until hood measures 7 ins. (18 cm) not including front band.
Sc BO 25 (26, 25, 24) sts beg of next 2 rows. 16 (16, 18, 20) sts rem.
Ss until this section measures 8 (8, 7½, 7½) ins. [20.5, 20.5, 19, 19 cm]
Sc BO rem sts.

Finishing
Block all pieces, and using mattress stitch sew together in this order:
• Sew shoulder seams together
• Sew sleeve cap (top) to armhole(s), easing to fit.
• Sew sleeve seams and Body side seams.
• Sew back seams of hood.
• Locate center of hood back and center of body back at neckline. Using this as guideline, pin hood along back and front of neckline with hood bands at center of front neckline. Sew together.
• Weave in tails and trim excess.

Simple Shell

By Isela Phelps

This is the perfect top for that hot summer day when a sweater is just too much.

INTERMEDIATE

Materials

Knitting Loom

Regular gauge with at least 64 pegs [Sample uses DA baby afghan loom regular gauge]

 ### Yarn

8 (9, 10, 11, 12, 13, 15) ozs [227, 255, 284, 312, 340, 367, 425 g] of Aran weight yarn [Sample uses Sublime cashmere merino silk Aran, 75% extra-fine merino, 20% silk, 5% cashmere 3½ oz (50 g), 94 yds. (86 m) in 16 Mulberry]

Tools

Knitting tool
Tapestry needle
Row counter (optional)

Size(s)

Misses 6 (8, 10, 12, 14, 16, 18) [UK 10, 12, 14, 16, 18, 20] sample shown in size 6 [UK 10]

Finished Bust Measurements 30 (31, 32.5, 34, 36, 38, 40) ins. [76, 79, 83, 86, 91, 97, 102 cm]

Gauge

13 sts and 19 rows to 4 ins. (10 cm)

Seed st patt

Row 1: *K1, p1; rep from * to the end of row.
Row 2: *P1, k1; rep from * to the end of row.
Rep these 2 rows to form the patt.

DIRECTIONS (make 2)

Co 50 (52, 54, 56, 58, 60, 64) sts. Work rows 1–6 (1–6, 1–6, 1–8, 1–8, 1–10, 1–10) in seed st.
Next: work in St st, until item measures 12 (12, 12.5, 13, 13.5, 14.5, 15) ins. [30, 30, 32, 33, 34, 37, 38 cm] from co edge. (If you want a longer top, work more rows in this area).

All sizes:
BO 2 sts at beg of next 4 rows.
Sizes 12, 14, 16, 18:
BO 1 st at beg of foll 4 rows.

All sizes:
Work 10 (10, 12, 12, 14, 16, 16) rows in St st.
Work 6 (6, 6, 8, 8, 10, 12) rows of seed st.

All sizes:
Work first 6 sts in seed st. Attach another ball of yarn. BO 30 (28, 30, 32, 34, 36, 40) sts, work last 6 sts in seed st.

Cont working on both armbands in seed st, until armband measures: 3 (3, 3, 3½, 3½, 3½, 3½ ins.) [7.5, 7.5, 9, 9, 9, 9 cm]. BO with open method.

Finishing

Block lightly.
Assemble by sewing the sides first. Join it on the first row after the seed st border. After the sides are sewn, sew the shoulders.

Attach 3 buttons to the front top seed st band (choose the side you like best to be the front).

V-Neck Vest

By Isela Phelps

When cold weather comes and you need mobility and a coat is just too bulky, pull out this vest and keep warm while still being able to move around.

INTERMEDIATE

Materials

Knitting Loom

Regular Gauge knitting loom with at least 52 pegs [Sample knit using DA baby afghan regular gauge]

Yarn

900 yds. (823 m) of Aran-weight yarn (used doubled throughout patt) [Sample uses Sublime yarn, 75% extra fine merino wool, 20% silk, 5% cashmere, 1¾ oz (50 g) 94 yds. (85 m) in 0018 gray

Tools

Knitting tool
Tapestry needle

Sizes

Children sizes xs (s, m, l) Sample shown in largest size
Finished Chest Measurements:
30 (34, 36, 38) ins. [76, 86, 91, 97 cm]

Gauge

12 sts and 18 rows to 4 ins. (10 cm)

Rib St

Row 1: *K2, p2; rep from * to the end
Row 2: *P2, k2; rep from * to the end

Pattern notes

Double-strand the yarn throughout patt.

Back

Co 40 (44, 48, 52) sts.
Next: Work 8 rows in Rib St.
Next: Change to St st and work even for 8.5 (10½, 12, 13) in. [21.5, 26.5, 30, 33 cm] or until the desired length is reached.

Armhole shaping

Next: BO 2sts at beg of foll 4 rows.
Next: K2, ssk, k to last 4sts, k2tog, k2.

Larger two sizes:

Next: K2, ssk, k to last 4sts, k2tog, k2.

Sts rem on the loom: 30 (34, 36, 40).
Next: Work in St st until armhole depth measures: 6 (7, 7½, 8) ins. [15, 18, 19, 20.5 cm].
BO loosely.

Front

Follow same instructions as for back until armhole shaping is completed. Yarn should be at right side of the loom, ready to begin working from right to left direction.

V–neck shaping

Work both sides at the same time.
Next row: K12 (k14, k15, k17) k2tog, k1.
Attach second ball of yarn and work the second side as follows: K1, ssk, k to the end.
Next row: K all sts.
*Next row:** K to last 3 sts of this side k2tog, k1. Drop yarn and pick up the other yarn and work the second side as follows: K1, ssk, k to the end.
Next row: K all sts*.
Rep from * to * until 8 (8, 8, 9) sts rem. BO all sts.

Armbands

Co 48, 52, 56, 60 sts.
Work in Rib St for 1 in. (2.5 cm).
BO loosely.

Finishing

Block all pieces
Assemble as follows: Sew the shoulders first, and then the side seams. Lastly, sew armbands to the body.

Pi Sweater Coat

By Kathy Norris

A loom-knit version of the popular circle sweater. Worked in short rows, the body is knitted as one piece with one seam at the bottom of the sweater. The sleeves are knitted separately and fitted into the armholes.

■■■□
INTERMEDIATE

Materials

Knitting Loom

Large gauge loom with at least 51 (57, 61) pegs (Long Blue Knifty Knitter was used in sample)

Yarn

Noro Cotton Hill 15 (16, 17) skeins, 99 yds. (90.5 m) 1¾ oz (50 g) in 3

Tools

Knitting tool
Crochet hook
Tapestry needle
Stitch markers

Sizes

Small (medium, large)
Bust: 34–36 (38–40, 42–44) ins.
[86–91, 97–102, 107–112 cm]
Patt is written for small, with medium and large in parentheses

Gauge

10 sts and 11 rows to 4 ins. (10 cm) (e-wrap knit st)

Pattern notes

When instructed to knit a peg that has more than one loop, wrap and knit the peg so that one loop is left.

Body

Co 51 (57, 61) sts.
Wy is now at peg #1. The placement of st markers on pegs 2 to 7 will help remind you that these pegs are purled the first row and every other row thereafter.

Panel instructions:

*Panel row 1: Sl1, p6, W&T next peg.
Panel row 2: SS7.
Panel row 3: Sl1, p6, SS2, W&T next peg.
Panel row 4: SS9.
Rep rows 1 to 4, 40 (46, 50) more times, increasing sts on rows 3 and 4 by 1 each time until you reach 49 (55, 59) in row 4.*
Rep Panel Instructions * to * once more.
Next row: Sl1, p6, W&T next peg.
Next row: SS7.
Next row: Sl1, p6, SS44 (50, 54) **.
Next row: Sl 1, SS50 (56, 60).

Armhole panel instructions

* Work panel rows 1–4 again.
Rep panel rows 1–4: 19 (21, 23) more times, increasing sts on rows 3 and 4 by 1 each time until you reach 28 (30, 32) SSs in row 4.

Work Panel Rows 1–2.
Sl1, p6, SS22 (24, 26); lift loop from peg where wy is and put on crochet hook; work sc BO for this loop and next 2 loops so that there are 3 empty pegs; put loop from crochet hook onto next peg that has a loop and bring bottom loop over top loop; W&T next peg. SS1.

Armhole row 1: Sl1, SS2, W&T next.
Armhole row 2: SS3.
Rep armhole rows 1 and 2: 14 (15, 16) more times increasing sts on both rows by 1 each time until you reach 17 (18, 19) in row 2. Cut wy and attach yarn to loom in order to work pegs 1 to 28 (30, 32).
Armhole row 3: Sl 1, p6, W&T next.
Armhole row 4: SS7.
Armhole row 5: Sl1, p6, SS21 (23, 25).
Armhole row 6: Sl1 SS27 (29, 31).
Rep Armhole rows 3–6: 14 (15, 16) more times.
Rep Armhole Rows 3 and 4.
Sl 1, p6, SS21 (23, 25), SS co next 3 empty pegs; SS18 (19, 20), W&T next peg. SS 49 (52, 55)
Panel row 5: Sl 1, p6, W&T next.
Panel row 6: SS 7.
Panel row 7: Sl 1, p6, SS 43 (46, 49), W&T next.
Panel row 8: SS 50 (53, 56).

Rep Panel Rows 5–8, 0 (3, 4) more times, increasing sts on rows 7 and 8 by 1 each time until you reach 50 (56, 60) in row 8.*
Work panel instructions * to *.
Next row: Sl 1, p 6, W&T next peg.
Next row: SS7.
Next row: Sl 1, p 6, SS 44 (50, 54).
Next row: Sl 1, SS 50 (56, 60).

Work "Armhole Panel Instructions" * to *.
Work panel instructions * to **
Sc BO peg 51 (57, 61) to peg 1.

Sleeves (make 2)
Co 26 (26, 28) with crochet cast-on.
Row 1: Sl1, *k1, p1*; rep * to * to end of row.
Rep last instruction for 12 more rows, slipping first st of each row, knit the knit sts and purl the purl sts.
Hint: St markers will help to identify which pegs to knit or purl.

Next: *Sl1, SS to end of row for 4 rows.
Sl1, m1, SS until 1 peg with loop is left, m1, SS1.*
Rep * to * 10 (11, 11) more times.
Sl 1, SS to end of row for 3 (1, 1) row(s).
BO with basic bind-off method.

Finishing
The body of Pi will need one seam. With right side facing up, line up the edges of the bottom of the circle. Use mattress st to seam from bottom edges to where the co-tail is at center of circle. There will be a small open gap at the center. Close this gap with gathered BO, passing yarn through edge sts of the gap and pulling yarn tight.
With wrong sides facing, fold sleeve lengthwise. Pin into armhole, insuring sleeve seam is pointed "downward" (in the direction of the body seam). The armholes of the body will appear larger then the sleeve armhole edge. The sts will draw in on the armhole of the body as you seam it to the sleeve. Use mattress st to seam sleeve to body and to seam sleeve closed along arm. Rep for other sleeve.

Cozy Mitts

By Isela Phelps

The yarn makes these mitts special! It is soft to the touch and warm. They work up fast—in less than three hours you can make a pair for you—then one for each of your friends.

INTERMEDIATE

Materials

Knitting Loom

Large gauge loom with a minimum of 24 pegs.
[Sample uses round Blue Knifty Knitter Loom]

Yarn

100 yds. (91.5 m) of bulky-weight yarn
[Sample uses Berroco Plush, 100% nylon, 1¾ oz (50 g) 90 yds. (83 m) in light pink]

Tools

Knitting tool
Tapestry needle

Size

Adult female

Gauge

12 sts and 20 rows to 4 ins. (10 cm)

Directions (Make 2)
Co 24 sts, join into the round.
Rnds 1–20: work in St st (knit all rounds).

Thumb

Working as a flat panel on pegs 1–8, work 20 rows (at the end of the 20 rows, yarn should be by peg 1).

Body

Work 22 rounds in St st.
BO with gathering method.

Finishing

Thread tapestry needle and seam the sides of the thumb with mattress st.

Man's Colorwork Hat

By Isela Phelps

Making hats for men can be tricky—they want something plain, and non-frilly. The basic hat pattern below will allow you to make a simple yet classic hat. If you want to get a little creative, include the colorwork and create a fun hat.

INTERMEDIATE

Materials

Knitting Loom

Round knitting loom with a peg multiple of 5 (motif is a multiple of 5 sts) [Adult Regular Gauge hat loom with 60 pegs by Décor Accents was used in sample]

Yarn

160 yds. (146 m) of MC; 50 yds. (46 m) CC [Sample uses Debbie Bliss Cashmerino Aran 55% merino wool, 33% microfiber, 12% cashmere, 1¾ oz (50 g) 98 yds. (90 m) in navy and gray

Tools

Knitting tool
Tapestry needle
Row counter (optional)

Size(s)

Adult size male
Head circumference: 22 ins. (56 cm).
You can adapt the st patt to any other knitting loom with a multiple of 5 pegs.

Gauge

12 sts and 20 rows to 4 ins. (10 cm) in St st

Pattern notes

• Use 2 strands of yarn as one throughout patt.

• Read the chart starting at Row 1 on the lower right. Cont reading each row starting at the right side. When working chart, carry colors loosely together at back of work across a maximum of 3 sts. When carrying colors across more than 3 sts, weave it over and under the other color at every fourth st or at center point of sts it passes over. Remember yarn dominance—carry the background color above, reach under the background color for the foreground color. Maintain this yarn dominance throughout the patt. If making the basic version with no colorwork, ignore color changes and follow the patt to the end, omitting all color changes.

5	4	3	2	1		Key
					6	☐ knit
	●	●	●	●	5	● color
●	●				4	
●				●	3	
	●	●	●	●	2	
					1	

Directions

Place st markers 5 spaces apart: each colorwork patt rep takes 5 sts, place the markers to help you keep track of where you are on the chart.

Using MC: Co 60 sts (or a multiple of 5 sts), join in the round.

Rnd 1: *K2, p2; rep from * to the end of round.

Rep Rnd 1 until brim measures 2½ ins. (6.5 cm) from co edge.

Next: Work 1 in. (2.5 cm) in St st (knit all rounds).

[If making non-colorwork version, cont until item measures 8 in. (20.5 cm). Go straight to crown decreases section.]

Next 6 rounds: Work the 6 rounds from chart. (motif should fit 12 times around the loom, if using a 60 peg loom)

Next: Knit in St st for 4 ins. (10 cm) (Hat should measure about 8 in. (20.5 cm) from cast-on edge).

Crown Decreases

Next: K2tog all around (move st from peg 1 to peg 2, move st from peg 3 to peg 4.) Cont around the knitting loom in this manner.

BO rem sts with gather removal method.

Cables Beret

By Isela Phelps

A classic with a little cable twist! The beret below is constructed in four panels—try it with the cables or the non-cabled version.

INTERMEDIATE

Materials

Knitting Loom

Large gauge knitting loom with at least 24 pegs [Sample used Red Knifty Knitter by Provo Craft]

Yarn

250 yds. (228.5 m) of bulky-weight yarn [Sample uses GGH Aspen, 1¾ oz (50 g), 63 yds. (57 m) 50% merino, 50% microfiber in 24 teal]

Tools

Knitting tool
Tapestry needle
Cable needle
Stitch holder.

Size

Adult female (fits heads up to 21 ins. (53 cm) in circumference)

Gauge

12 sts and 18 rows to 4 ins. (10 cm)

Cables version (make 4 panels)

Brim

Co 12 sts.
Rows 1, 3, 5, 7: K.
Rows 2, 4, 6, 8: P.
Row 7: *K1, yo; rep from * to the end of row (24 sts).

Body (continuing from the brim)
Row 1: K all sts.
Row 2, 4, 5: K8, p2, k4, p2, k8.
Row 3: K8, p2, 4-st LC, p2, k8.
Rep Rows 2–5: 6 times (or until item measures 5 in. (12.5 cm) from co edge). End on a Row 4.
Next row: K1, ssk, k5, p2, k4, p2, k5, k2tog, k1.
Next row: K7, p2, k4, p2, k7.
Next row: K1, ssk, k4, p2, 4-st LC, p2, k4, k2tog, k1.
Next row: K6, p2, k4, p2, k6.
Next row: K1, ssk, k3, p2, k4, p2, k3, k2tog, k1.
Next row: K5, p2, k4, p2, k5.
Next row: K1, ssk, k2, p2, 4-st LC, p2, k2, k2tog, k1.
Next row: K4, p2, k4, p2, k4.
Next row: K1, ssk, k1, p2, k4, p2, k1, k2tog, k1.
Next row: K3, p2, k4, p2, k3.
Next row: K1, ssk, p2, 4-st LC, p2, k2tog, k1.
Next row: K2, p2, k4, p2, k2.
Next row: K1, ssk, p1, k4, p1, k2tog, k1.
Next row: K2, p1, k4, p1, k2.
Next row: K1, p2tog, 4-st LC, p2tog, k1.
Next row: K1, p1, k4, p1, k1.
Next row: K1, ssk, k2, k2tog, k1.
Next row: K6.
Next row: K1, ssk, k2tog, k1.
Next row: K4.
Next row: Ssk, k2tog.
Take rem two sts and place them on a st holder.

Plain Version (make 4 panels)

Brim

Co 12 sts
Row 1, 3, 5, 7: K.
Row 2, 4, 6, 8: P.
Row 7: *K1, yo; rep from * to the end of row (24 sts total).

Body

Row 1: K.
Rep Row 1 until item measures 5 in. (12.5 cm) from cast-on edge. End ready to begin an odd side row (yarn should be by right side of loom).
* **Next row:** K1, ssk, knit to last 3 sts, k2tog, k1.
Next row: K all sts *.
Rep from * to * until only 2 sts rem.

Finishing

Take rem two sts and place them on a st holder. Block and then sew together the four panels.
To join at the top: thread tapestry needle through the 8 live sts, gather the top closed.
Work a 2-st I-cord that is about 22 ins. (56 cm) long. Pass it through the eyelets made by the yarn-overs. The sample shows the I-cord passed through every other eyelet.

PART IV
Sock Drawer

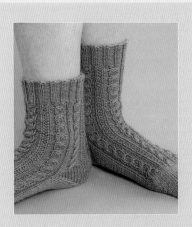

Family of Basic Socks

By Isela Phelps

Use the following basic sock pattern and get a kick start on your sock knitting for the entire family.

INTERMEDIATE

Materials

Knitting Loom

Extra small—48 peg extra-fine gauge knitting loom, 5 ins. (12.5 cm) [DA toddler EFG]

Small—56 peg extra fine gauge knitting loom 7 ins. (18 cm) [DA child EFG]

Medium—64 peg extra fine gauge knitting loom. 9 ins. (23 cm) [DA adult EFG]

Large—72 peg extra fine gauge knitting loom, 10 ins. 25.5 cm) [DA adult EFG]

 Yarn

150–350 yds. (137–320 m) of sock-weight yarn [Louet Gems Fingering Weight 100% merino wool, 185 yds. (169 m) 50g in Caribbean Blue, used in small size shown]

Notions

Knitting tool
Tapestry needle
2 dpn size 1 (2.25 mm)

Sizes

Foot circumference 5, 7, 8, 10 ins. (12, 18, 20, 25.5 cm). Pattern can be adapted to any other loom with a multiple of 4.

Gauge

18 sts and 24 rows to 2 ins. (5 cm) in St st (knit all rows)

Pattern notes

Clockwise direction around loom.

Pattern St
Rib

Key

● **knit** knit st
□ **purl** purl st

Directions (make 2)

Cast on 48 (56, 64, 72) sts with the ch-co method or the cable-co method, join in the rnd.

Cuff

Work 8 (10, 12, 14) rnds of rib st.

Leg

Work in St st until leg measures 4 (5, 6.5, 7) ins. (10, 12.5, 16.5, 18 cm) from cast-on edge.

Begin Heel

Note: Done as a flat panel using short-rows.

* Working on half the loom pegs, place markers on pegs 1 and 24 (1 and 28; 1 and 32; 1 and 36).

Row 1: Knit across to 1 peg before marker. Wrap peg with marker. The last st is now wrapped and rems unworked. Turn.

Row 2: Knit across row to 1 peg before first peg (peg with marker).

Wrap peg 1. This st is now wrapped and rems unworked. Turn.

Row 3: Knit across the row until the peg before the last wrapped peg. W&T.

Row 4: Knit across to the peg before the last peg wrapped. W&T. Repeat rows 3 and 4 until the 8 (8, 10, 12) middle sts (between markers) remain unwrapped.

Reverse short-row shaping (2nd half of heel shape)

Row 1: Work across to the next wrapped peg. Knit the loop tog with the wrap (treat them as 1 loop). Take the st off the next peg (peg 23) and wrap the peg. This peg now has 2 wraps on it, plus the loop. Turn.

Row 2: Knit across to the next wrapped peg. Knit the loop tog with the wrap (treat them as 1 loop). Take the st off the next peg and wrap the peg. This peg now has 2 wraps on it plus the loop. Turn. Repeat Rows 1 and 2 until you have worked all but the pegs with the st markers. These two pegs should remain unworked. Yarn will be by peg 2. *

Sock foot

Worked in the round.

Next row: Work in St st until sock sole measures 1 (1, 1½, 1½) ins. (2.5, 2.5, 4, 4 cm) less than the desired length.

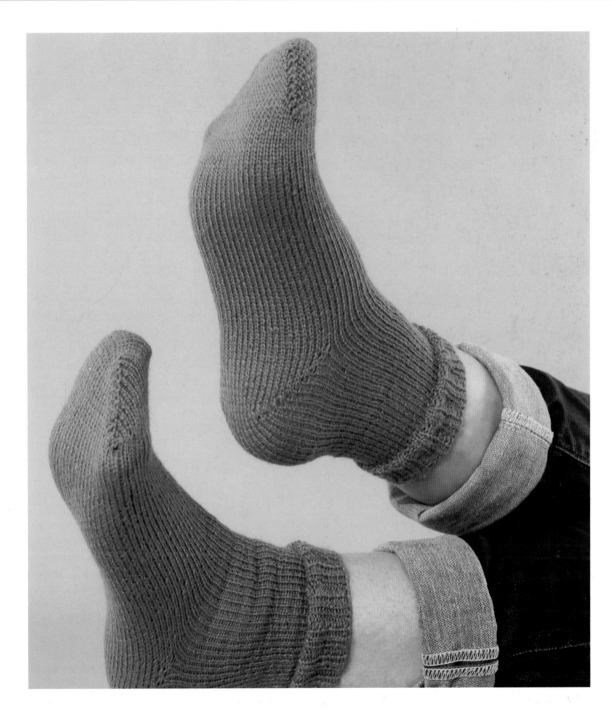

Begin toe

Working a short-row toe is the same as knitting a short-row heel. Work on the first half of loom sts and foll the short-row shaping instructions (from * to *). This time, cont knitting until you have worked the sts with the peg markers. The pegs from marker to marker should have one loop on them.

Finishing

Remove sts from loom as folls:
Place on dpn 1: sts from pegs 24–1 (28–1; 32–1; 36–1)
Place on dpn 2: sts from pegs 25–48 (29–56; 33–64; 37–72)

Sts are now prepared to graft closed. Foll grafting instructions to close the toe (see page 131).
To finish, weave all yarn tail ends. Block lightly.

Crabapple Socks

By Isela Phelps

Knit the cuff a little differently and add some interest to your socks. The pretty cabled rib is unusual and gives this basic sock pattern a lift.

INTERMEDIATE

Materials

Knitting Loom

64 peg extra-fine gauge knitting loom [9 ins. (23 cm) DA Adult EFG used in sample]

 Yarn

250–350 yds. (228–320 m) of sock-weight yarn per pair [Louet Gems Fingering Weight 100% merino wool, 185 yds. (169 m) per 50 g in Crabapple used in sample]

Notions

Knitting tool
Tapestry needle
2 dpn size 1 (2.25 mm)
peg markers

Size(s)

Shown 8 ins. (20 cm) foot circumference
To adapt pattern to smaller/larger loom: pattern can be adapted to any other loom with a peg multiple of 4

Gauge

18 sts and 24 rows to 2 ins. (5 cm) in St st (knit all rows)

Pattern notes

Clockwise direction around loom.

Mock Cable Chart

	4	3	2	1	
	●	●	╳	╳	3
	●	●			2
	●	●			1

Key

	knit
●	purl
╳╳	Left Twist

Directions (make 2)

Cast on 64 sts with the chain cast on method or the cable cast on method, join in the rnd.

Cuff

Rnds 1–15: Foll mock cable chart, rows 1–3.

Leg

Work in St st until leg measures 4 (5, 6½) ins. (10, 12, 16.5 cm) from cast on edge.

Begin Heel

Note: The heel is worked as a flat panel using short-row shaping (done on half the loom pegs). Place peg markers on pegs 1 and 32.

* **Row 1:** Knit across to peg before marker (peg 31). Wrap peg with marker. The last st is now wrapped and rem unworked. Turn.

Row 2: Knit across row to 1 peg before first peg (peg with marker). Wrap peg 1. This st is now wrapped and rems unworked. Turn.

Row 3: Knit across the row until the peg before the last wrapped peg. W&T.

Row 4: Knit across to the peg before the last peg wrapped. W&T. Repeat Rows 3 and 4, until the 10 middle sts (between markers) remain unwrapped.

Reverse short-row shaping (2nd half of heel shape)

Row 1: Work across to the next wrapped peg (22). Knit the loop tog with the wrap (treat them as 1 loop). Take the st off the next peg and wrap the peg. This peg now has 2 wraps on it, plus the loop. Turn.

Row 2: Knit across to the next wrapped peg. Knit the loop tog with the wrap (treat them as 1 loop). Take the st off the next peg and wrap the peg. This peg now has 2 wraps on it plus the loop. Turn.

Repeat Rows 1 and 2 until you have worked all but the pegs with the st markers. These two pegs should remain unworked. Yarn will be by peg 2. *

Sock Foot

(Worked in the round)

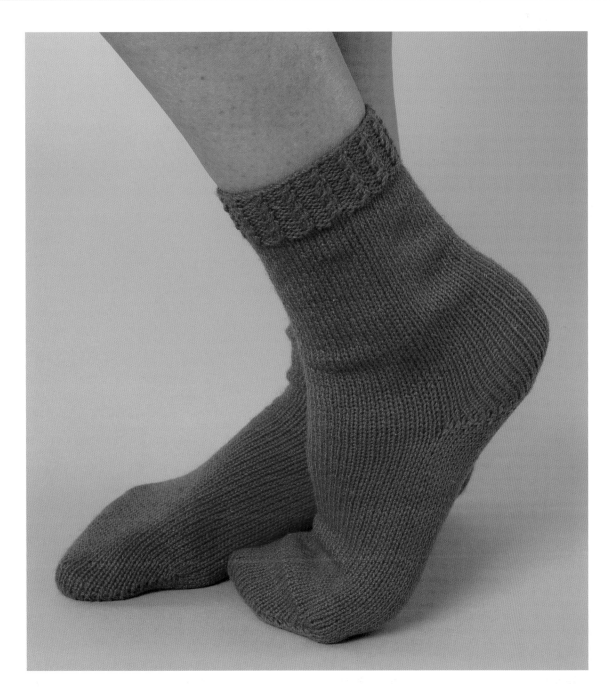

Next: Work in St st until sock sole measures 1½ ins. (4 cm) less than the desired length.

Begin Toe

Working a short-row toe is the same as knitting a short-row heel. Work on the first half of loom sts and foll the short-row shaping instructions (from * to *). This time, cont knitting until you have worked the sts with the peg markers. The pegs from marker to marker should have one loop on them.

Finishing

Remove sts from loom as folls: Place sts 32–1 on one dpn.

Place sts 33–64 on second dpn. Sts are now prepared to graft closed. Foll the grafting instructions on p 131 to close the toe. Weave all yarn tail ends. Block lightly.

Lace Panel Socks

By Isela Phelps

A simple lace panel is inserted into the front area of this sock pattern to bring a little attention to your handknits.

INTERMEDIATE

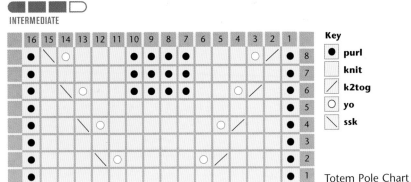

16	15	14	13	12	11	10	9	8	7	6	5	4	3	2	1	
●	\	○				●	●	●	●			○	/		●	8
●						●	●	●	●						●	7
●	\	○				●	●	●	●			○	/		●	6
●															●	5
●			\	○						○	/				●	4
●															●	3
●					\	○			○	/					●	2
●															●	1

Key
- ● purl
- □ knit
- / k2tog
- ○ yo
- \ ssk

Totem Pole Chart

Materials

Knitting Loom

64 peg extra-fine gauge knitting loom, 9 ins. (23 cm) or with a multiple of 4 pegs [DA Adult EFG used in sample]

1 SUPER FINE

Yarn

350–400 yds. (320, 366 cm) of sock-weight yarn. [Debbie Bliss Baby Cashmerino, 55% merino wool, 33% microfiber, 12% cashmere, 137 yds. (125 m) per 50 g in shade 601 was used in sample]

Notions

Knitting tool
Tapestry needle
Two dpn size 1 (2.25 mm)

Sizes

Shown in 8 ins. (20 cm) foot circumference, US size 6.5. To adapt pattern to smaller/larger loom: pattern can be adapted to any other loom with a peg multiple of 4

Gauge

16 sts and 24 rows to 2 ins. (5 cm) in St st (knit all rows)

Pattern notes

Knit in a clockwise direction arnd knitting loom.

Directions (make 2)

Cast on 64 sts with the chain cast on method or the cable cast-on method, join in the rnd.

Cuff

Rnds 1–8: *K2, p2; rep from * to the end of rnd.

Leg

Rnds 1-8: *K8, foll Totem Pole Chart, k40.
Repeat Leg rnds 1–16 until item reaches 6.5 ins. (16.5 cm). End on a rnd 8 of Totem Pole Chart.

Begin Heel

(Flat panel using short-rows)
* Short-row shaping (done on 32 sts). Place pegs markers on peg 1 and 32.
Row 1: Knit across to peg 31. Wrap peg 32. The last st is now wrapped and rems unworked. Turn.
Row 2: Knit across row to the first peg. Wrap peg 1. This st is now wrapped and rems unworked. Turn.
Row 3: Knit across the row until the peg before the last wrapped peg. W&T.
Row 4: Knit across to the peg before the last peg wrapped. W&T.

Repeat rows 3 and 4 until the 10 middle sts remain unwrapped.

Reverse short-row shaping (2nd half of heel shape)

Row 1: Work across to the next wrapped peg (peg 22). Knit the loop tog with the wrap (treat them as 1 loop). Take the next st off the peg (peg 23) and wrap the peg. This peg now has 2 wraps on it, plus the loop. Turn.
Row 2: Knit across to the next wrapped peg (peg 11). Knit the loop tog with the wrap (treat them as 1 loop). Take the next st off the peg (peg 10) and wrap the peg. This peg now has 2 wraps on it plus the loop. Turn.

Repeat Rows 1 and 2 until you have worked all but the pegs with the st markers, pegs 1 and 32, which

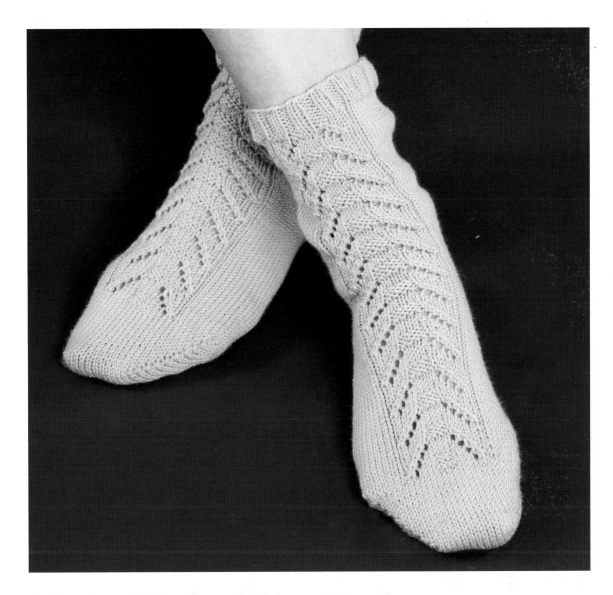

should remain unworked. Yarn will be by peg 2. *

Sock Foot

Worked in the rnd

Rnd 1: K64

Repeat rnds 1 until sock sole measures 1.5 ins. (4 cm) less than desired length.

Begin Toe

Working a short-row toe is the same as knitting a short-row heel. Work on the first 32 sts and foll the short-row shaping instructions (from * to *). This time, cont knitting until you have worked the sts with the peg markers. The pegs from marker to marker should have one loop on them.

Remove sts from loom as folls:
Place on dpn 1: Sts from pegs 32–1.
Place on dpn 2: Sts from pegs 33–64.
Foll grafting instructions to close the toe (see page 131).

Finishing

Weave in all ends. Block lightly.

Lacy Socks

By Tracey Carsto

A simple lace pattern looks effective with this special space-dyed yarn. The yarn changes color so you don't have to.

INTERMEDIATE

	4	3	2	1	Key
				4	☐ knit
				3	◯ yo
				2	⦸ p2tog
	✕	⦸	◯	1	✕ No St

Pattern notes
Knit in a clockwise direction.

Stitch Pattern
Rnd 1: *K, yo, p2tog, p* repeat.
Rnd 2–4: Knit all pegs.

Directions:
Co in the rnd with the chain cast-on method.

Cuff
Rnds 1–20: *K2, P2; rep from * to the end of rnd.

Leg
Rnd 1: K, yo, p2tog, p.
Rnds 2–4: Knit all sts.
Repeat rnds 1–4 until sock measures 6 ins. (15 cm) or desired length.
Begin heel
Short-row shaping (done on 32 sts). * Place pegs markers on peg 1 and 32.
Row 1: Knit across to peg 31. W peg 32. The last st is now wrapped and rem unworked. Turn.
Row 2: Knit across row to the first peg. W peg 1. This st is now wrapped and rem unworked. Turn.
Row 3: Knit across the row until the peg before the last wrapped peg. W&T.

Row 4: Knit across to the peg before the last peg wrapped. W&T. Repeat Rows 3 and 4, until the 10 middle sts remain unwrapped.

Reverse short-row shaping (2nd half of heel shape)
Row 1: Work across to the next wrapped peg (peg 22). Knit the loop tog with the wrap (treat them as 1 loop). Take the next st off the peg (peg 23) and wrap the peg. This peg now has 2 wraps on it, plus the loop. Turn.
Row 2: Knit across to the next wrapped peg (peg 11). Knit the loop tog with the wrap (treat them as 1 loop). Take the next st off the peg (peg 10) and wrap the peg. This peg now has 2 wraps on it plus the loop. Turn.
Repeat Rows 1 and 2 until you have worked all but the pegs with the st markers, pegs 1 and 32, (pegs 1 and 32 should remain unworked). Yarn will be by peg 2.
End of Heel*

Sock foot (worked in the rnd)
Rnds 1–4: K32, foll st pattern on rem 32 sts.
Repeat rnds 1–4 until sock sole measures 1½ ins. (4 cm) less than desired length.
Next: Work 2 rnds of St st.

Begin Toe
Work on the first 32 sts and foll the short-row shaping instructions (from * to *). This time, cont knitting until you have worked the sts with the

Materials

Knitting Loom

64 peg extra fine gauge knitting loom, 9 ins. (23 cm) [DA Adult EFG used in sample] To re-create the pattern, you will need a knitting loom with a peg count multiple of 4

Yarn

100% superwash merino fingering weight with a put up of 4 oz (114 g) 420 yds. (128 m) 350–400 yds. (320, 366 m) of sock weight yarn [Louet Gems fingering-weight 100% merino wool, 185 yds. (169 m) per 50g in Aqua was used in sample]

Notions

Knitting tool, Tapestry needle
Two dpn size 1 (2.25 mm)

Size

Shown in 8 ins. (20 cm) foot circumference, US size 9. To adapt pattern to smaller/larger loom: pattern can be adapted to any other loom with a peg multiple of 4

Gauge

16 sts and 24 rows to 2 ins. (5 cm) in St st (knit all rows)

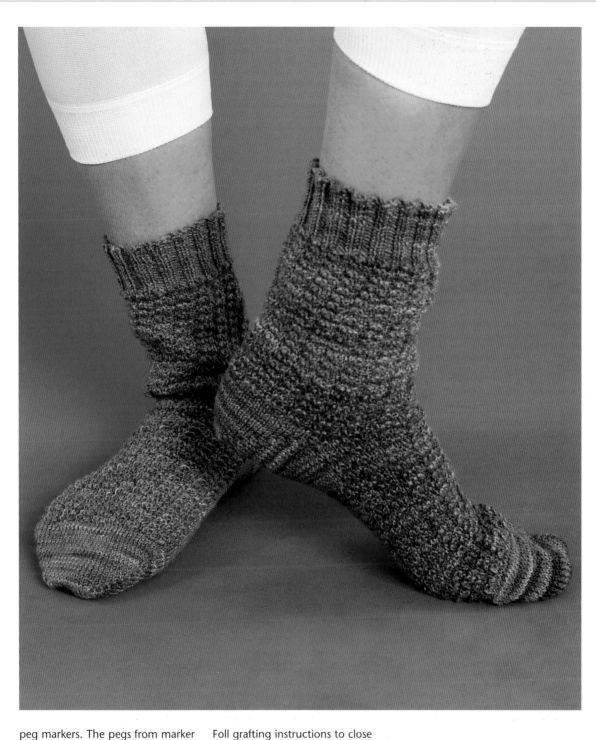

peg markers. The pegs from marker to marker should have one loop on them.

Remove sts from loom as folls:
Place on dpn 1: Sts from pegs 32–1.
Place on dpn 2: Sts from pegs 33–64.

Foll grafting instructions to close the toe.

Finishing

Weave in ends. Block lightly.

Garter Rib Socks

By Isela Phelps

These stylish unisex socks are easier to make than they look.

INTERMEDIATE

Materials

Knitting Loom

64 peg extra fine gauge knitting loom [9 ins. (23 cm) DA Adult EFG used in sample]

Yarn

1 SUPER FINE

350–400 yards of sock weight yarn. [Louet Gems fingering-weight 100% merino wool, 185 yds. (169 m) per 50 g Aqua was used in sample]

Notions

Knitting tool
Tapestry needle,
2 dpn size 1 (2.25 mm)
Stitch markers

Size

8 ins. (20 cm) foot circumference or use smaller/larger loom with a peg multiple of 4

Gauge

18 sts and 24 rows to 2 ins. (5 cm) St st (knit all rows)

Directions (make 2)

Co 64 sts with the chain cast on method or the cable co method, join in the rnd.

Cuff

Rnd 1–8: *K2, p2. Rep from * to the end of rnd.

Leg

Rnd 1: *K2, p2; rep from * to the end of rnd.
Rnd 2: Knit to the end of rnd.
Repeat leg rnds 1–2 until item reaches 6½ ins. (16.5 cm) ending on a rnd 2.

Begin heel

Note: The heel is worked as a flat panel using short-rows.
* Short-row shaping (done on 32 sts). Place pegs markers on peg 1 and 32.
Row 1: Knit across to peg 31. Wrap peg 32. Turn.
Row 2: Knit across row to the first peg. Wrap peg 1. Turn.
Row 3: Knit across the row until the peg before the last wrapped peg. W&T.
Row 4: Knit across to the peg before the last peg wrapped. W&T.
Repeat Rows 3 and 4, until the 10 middle sts remain unwrapped.

Reverse short-row shaping (2nd half of heel shape)
Row 1: Work across to the next wrapped peg (peg 22). Knit the loop tog with the wrap (treat them as 1 loop). Take the next st off peg

23 and W&T.
Row 2: Knit across to the next wrapped peg (peg 11). Knit the loop tog with the wrap (treat them as 1 loop). Take the next st off the peg (peg 10) and W&T.
Repeat Rows 1 and 2 until you have worked all but the pegs with the st markers (pegs 1 and 32). Pegs 1 and 32 should remain unworked. Yarn will be by peg 2. *

Sock foot (worked in the rnd)
Rnd 1: K32, *k2, p2, rep from * to the end of rnd.
Rnd 2: Knit to the end of rnd.
Repeat rnds 1–2 until sock sole measures 1.5 ins. (4 cm) less than desired length.
Next: Work 2 rnds of St st.

Begin toe

Work on the first 32 sts and foll the short-row shaping instructions (from * to *). This time, cont knitting until you have worked the sts with the peg markers. The pegs from marker to marker should have one loop on them.
Remove sts from loom as folls:
Place on dpn 1: Sts from pegs 32–1
Place on dpn 2: Sts from pegs 33–64.
Sts are now prepared to graft closed. Foll grafting instructions to close the toe.

Finishing

Weave in ends. Block lightly.

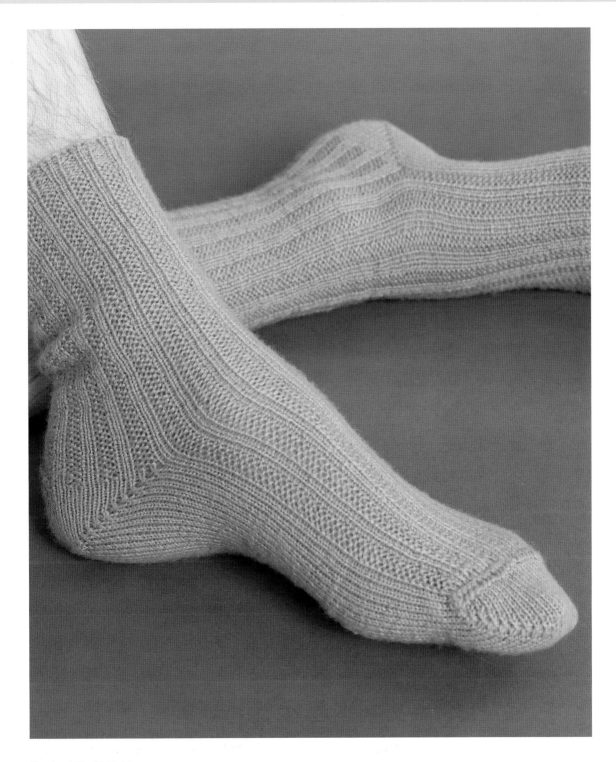

Garter Rib St Pattern

	4	3	2	1	
					3
	●	●			2

Key

☐ knit

● purl

Cables and Ribs Socks

By Evelyn H. Monsay

Knitted using sock yarn and an extra fine-gauge loom, these socks can be worn with any shoe. The details of cables and beaded ribs create socks that are both fancy and robust at the same time.

INTERMEDIATE

Materials

Knitting Loom

Extra-fine gauge sock loom with 64 pegs by Décor Accents.

Yarn

About 75 g of sock/fingering-weight yarn [Louet Gems fingering-weight (super fine), 100% merino wool, 1¾ oz (50 g), 185 yds. (169 m) in Lilac used in the sample]

Notions

Crochet hook
Knitting tool
Cable needle
Tapestry needle
Two dpn size 2 (2.75 mm)

Size

Women's medium

Gauge

8 sts and 10 rows to 1 in. (2.5 cm) with all rows in knit st

Pattern notes

The sock is worked clockwise. The overall pattern stitch involves a Cable Pattern unit assembled as follows:

Key

O = purl   X = knit

Peg Number

64	55 54 53	44 43 42	33 32	23 22 21	12 11 10	1
Cable Pattern 10 stitches x 6 rows	O X O X O X	Cable Pattern 10 stitches x 6 rows	O X O X O X	Cable Pattern 10 stitches x 6 rows	Cable Pattern 10 stitches x 6 rows	O X O X O X	Cable Pattern 10 stitches x 6 rows	O X O X O X	Cable Pattern 10 stitches x 6 rows

Front of leg/Top of foot   Back of leg

	10	9	8	7	6	5	4	3	2	1	
6			●	●				●	●		
5			●	●				●	●		
4			●	●	⟍⟋	⟍⊤		●	●		
3			●	●	SS	SS	SS	SS	●	●	
2								●	●		
1			●	●				●	●		

Key

▢ knit
● yo
⟋ single st
⟍⟋⟍⊤ c2 over 2 right

Cable pattern chart

The Cable Pattern is formed over blocks of ten pegs and six rows:

Written version of the pattern:

Row 1: [*(K1, P2, K4, P2, K1) K1*; repeat from * to *; K1, P2, K4, P2, K1] twice.

Row 2: [*(K1, P2, K4, P2, K1) P1*; repeat from * to *; K1, P2, K4, P2, K1] twice.

Row 3: [*(K1, P2, e4, P2, K1) K1*; repeat from * to *; K1, P2, e4, P2, K1] twice.

Row 4: [*(K1, P2, CB4, P2, K1) P1*; repeat from * to *; K1, P2, CB4, P2, K1] twice.

Row 5: Repeat Row 1.

Row 6: Repeat Row 2.

Cuff

Cast on 64 sts using the chain cast on method.
Rnd 1: *K2, P2; repeat from * to end of rnd.
Repeat Rnd 1 until cuff measures 1½ ins. (4 cm) from start.

Leg

Work in patt st, completing eight repetitions (48 rows). Item should measure approximately 6½ ins. (17 cm) from start.

Begin heel

* Short-row shaping is done on 32 sts. Place peg markers on pegs 1 and 32.

Row 1: Knit across to peg 31. Wrap peg 32. Turn.

Row 2: Knit across row to the first peg. Wrap peg 1. Turn.

Row 3: Knit across the row until the peg before the last wrapped peg. W&T.

Row 4: Knit across to the peg before the last peg wrapped. W&T. Repeat rows 3 and 4 until the 10 middle sts remain unwrapped.

Reverse short-row shaping (2nd half of heel shape)

Row 1: Work across to the next wrapped peg (peg 22). Knit the loop tog with the wrap (treat them as 1 loop). Take the next st off the peg (peg 23) and wrap the peg. This peg now has 2 wraps on it, plus the loop. Turn.

Row 2: Knit across to the next wrapped peg (peg 11). Knit the loop tog with the wrap (treat them as 1 loop). Take the next st off the peg (peg 10) and wrap the peg. This peg now has 2 wraps on it plus the loop. Turn.

Repeat Rows 1 and 2 until you have worked all but the pegs with the st markers, pegs 1 and 32, which should remain unworked. Yarn will be by peg 2. *

Foot

Work in St st (K all sts) on pegs 1 through 32, and cont in the Pattern St on pegs 33 through 64 until the piece measures approximately 8 ins. (20 cm) from the back of the heel. Feel free to adjust the length of the foot to fit, allowing approximately 2¼ in. (6 cm) for the toe.

Begin toe

Working a short-row toe is the same as knitting a short-row heel. Work on the first 32 sts and foll the short-row shaping instructions (from * to *). This time, cont knitting until you have worked the sts with the peg markers. The pegs from marker to marker should have one loop on them.

Remove sts from loom as folls:
Place on dpn 1: Sts from pegs 32–1
Place on dpn 2: Sts from pegs 33–64
Sts are now prepared to graft closed. Foll grafting instructions to close the toe (see page 131).

Finishing

Weave all yarn tail ends.
Block lightly.

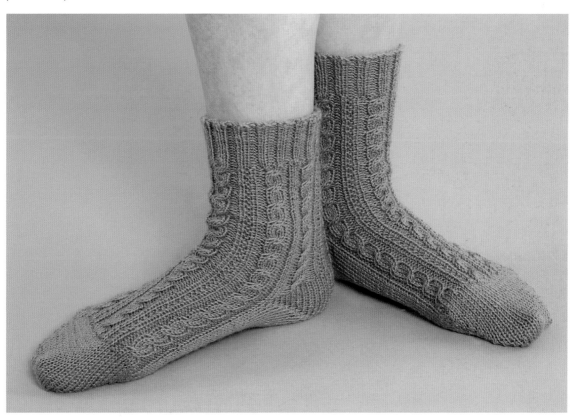

PART V
For Pets

Pooch Parka

By Bethany Dailey

Parade your pooch in style! Knit up this quick and easy parka for those cool evening walks, or just to provide some pampering for your pet, because even dogs love to have style.

INTERMEDIATE

Materials

Knitting Loom

Knifty Knitter Blue Loom (large gauge with at least 24 pegs)

Yarn

Worsted-weight yarn MC [104 yds. (94 m) Lion Brand Cotton Ease 1¾ oz (50 g), 50% cotton, 50% acrylic in Lime]

Bulky-weight yarn for trim, CC [36 yds. (33 m) Patons Pooch, 2.4 oz (70 g), 63% acrylic, 27% wool, 10% nylon in Teal Leaves]

Notions

Looming tool
J-10 (6 mm) crochet hook
Tapestry needle
Row counter
Large coordinating button

Size

Created for an extra small pooch. Measure your dog around the chest, and the length of body from base of neck to 3 in. (7.5 cm) from base of tail, and use the gauge to determine how the sts and rows will need to be adjusted. A shift up in the loom size may also be needed.

Gauge

16 sts and 11 rows to 4 in. (10 cm)

Single rib:
R1: *K1, p1; rep from * to the end.
Next rows: Knit the knit sts, purl the purled sts.

DIRECTIONS

CO 24 sts, join into the round.
Rnds 1–15: Work in single rib st.

Body

Row 16–20: CO holding 2 strands of your MC yarn. DS in the round. Do not cut yarn.
Row 21: CO your CC yarn and SS pegs 1–5.
***Note:** this first row will be KO 2 loops over 1.
Twist the MC around the CC by moving the MC over the top of the CC and all the way around.
DS pegs 6–24 using MC.
Row 22: Twist with CC on top and around, SS pegs 4–8. ***Note:** you will be skipping pegs 1–3 for now. Twist MC over the top of the CC and around and DS pegs 9–22. Twist CC over top and SS pegs 23–3.
Row 23: Move the loop from peg 2 to peg 3 and KO. Move this loop back to peg 2. Move the loop from peg 5 to peg 4 and KO. Move this loop back to peg 5. Pegs 3 and 4 will be empty. Twist CC over top and SS on pegs 5–8.
Twist MC over top and DS pegs 9–22.
Twist CC over top and SS pegs 23–2.

Rows 24–53: (Knitted flat) Work in patt.
Rows 54–59: SS using MC rem pegs.
BO with basic BO method.

Strap

Working on the outside of your jacket, find the 5 sts that mark approx. the back two-thirds of the MC portion, right before the CC. Place the "leg" of the sts closest to the CC up onto 5 pegs through the inside of your loom.
Rows 1–52: CO 2 strands of MC and DS 52 rows. *note: this strap will go around your dog's rib cage. Measure your dog, measure your finished jacket in width, and add 5 in. (12.5 cm) to find your strap length.
Row 53: Move the loop on peg #3 to peg #2 and KO. DS all pegs, except peg #3, which is now empty. Just carry the WY behind the peg and continue on.
Row 54: DS all 5 pegs. Peg #3 will only have one loop, and so will not be KO.
Row 55: Wrap all pegs loosely and KO 2 loops over 1 (peg 3 will be 1 over 1). BO with basic BO method. Whipstitch around the place where you decreased peg 3. This will be your button hole.
Sew the button to the other side of the jacket, 1 in. (2.5 cm) up from the CC edge.
Weave in ends, and trim.

Catnap Cozy

By Bethany Dailey

Your kitty will have sweet dreams in abundance while curled up in this fuzzy felted bed made just for him or her. Even the pickiest of felines won't be able to resist its cozy comforts!

INTERMEDIATE

Materials

Knitting Loom

Sample knit using both the Knifty Knitter red round loom (31 pegs) and the blue long loom (62 pegs). Any loom of similar size and large gauge could be substituted.

Yarn

Worsted-weight 100% wool [Patons Classic Merino 3½ oz (100 g) to 223 yd. (205 m). 5 balls old gold (MC); 1 ball each of leaf green (C1) and paprika (C2)

Notions

Knitting tool
J-10 (6 mm) crochet hook
High loft batting
Broom handle or 1½ ins. (4 cm)
   diameter dowel
Tapestry needle

Size

28 ins. (71 cm) in diameter

Gauge

4 ins. (10 cm) sq unfelted:
   12 sts x 13 rows
4 ins. (10 cm) sq felted:
   9 sts x 24 rows (may vary)

Pattern notes

- For felting you will need access to hot water, or washing machine, a tablespoon of laundry detergent, a pillowcase, and a pair or two of well-worn jeans
- The bed top of the cozy uses colorwork to achieve the fish and mouse designs. Follow the chart for details on how many rows of each color.
- Begin reading the chart at bottom right corner, right to left. Use a sticky note to keep your place.
- Color changes, are done by twisting the yarn over the top of the previous color, all the way around, and back up to wrap on peg. There is no need to trim the yarn used for your shapes in between rows, just carry it over behind the work and then create your twists.

Bed top

With MC, cast on 31sts and join in the round.
Follow chart below to begin color-work.

Option: if you prefer a plain color omit the color changes and work 190 rnds in color of choice.

- This patt will be rep 4 more times, with these color changes:
- **Rep 1:** main color: C2, mouse: , fish: MC
- **Rep 2:** main color: C1, mouse: MC, fish: C2
- **Rep 3:** main color: MC, mouse: C2, fish: C1
- **Rep 4:** main color: C2, mouse: C1, fish: MC
- SS 6 more rows using the main color.

*Note: If you prefer another color patt, just make sure it totals 196 rows.
BO by sewing the working yarn through each loop around the loom and knotting.

Bed base (knit as a flat panel)
CO to your blue long loom, beginning with pegs 21–40. This will let you work evenly on the loom as you increase and decrease.
Rows 1–40: SS. At the end of each row, add one peg. By row 40 you will have 60 pegs with loops on them.
Rows 41–60: Work even in SS.
Row 61: Move the loop on peg #2 to peg #1, KO. Move the loop back to peg 2. SS 59 rem pegs.
Rows 62–100: rep row 61, alternating sides for decrease. By row 100, you will be back to 20 pegs with loops.
Without BO rep entire procedure again to make the second layer of the bed.
BO by sewing your working yarn through each loop and knotting. Stitch your base sides together, leaving 12 ins. (30 cm) open.

31	30	29	28	27	26	25	24	23	22	21	20	19	18	17	16	15	14	13	12	11	10	9	8	7	6	5	4	3	2	1	
																			MC												38
																		MC	MC	MC											37
																	MC	MC	MC	MC	MC										36
																MC	MC	MC	MC	MC	MC	MC									35
																MC	MC	MC	MC	MC	MC	MC									34
																MC	MC	MC	MC	MC	MC	MC									33
																MC	MC	MC	MC	MC	MC	MC									32
																	MC	MC	MC	MC	MC										31
																	MC	MC	MC	MC	MC										30
																		MC	MC	MC											29
																				MC												28
																		MC	MC	MC												27
																MC	MC	MC	MC	MC											26
																	MC				MC										25
																MC						MC									24
																															23
																															22
																															21
																								C2							20
																							C2	C2							19
																						C2	C2	C2							18
																					C2	C2	C2	C2							17
																				C2	C2	C2	C2	C2							16
																		C2	C2	C2	C2	C2	C2	C2							15
																		C2	C2	C2	C2	C2	C2	C2							14
																			C2	C2	C2	C2	C2	C2							13
																			C2	C2	C2	C2	C2	C2							12
																		C2	C2	C2	C2	C2	C2								11
																		C2	C2	C2	C2	C2	C2								10
																		C2	C2	C2	C2	C2									9
																			C2	C2	C2	C2									8
																				C2	C2	C2									7
																				C2				C2	C2						6
																				C2				C2							5
																			C2	C2	C2										4
																															3
																															2
																															1

FELTING

Make sure you plan to felt your Catnap Cozy when you have the time to complete the finishing steps, as it is best to assemble it while it is still damp. This way the bed will dry while in its permanent shape. The sample was felted for 15 minutes, with 2 pairs of well-worn jeans thrown into the washing machine for extra agitation.

FINISHING

- When you remove your two project pieces from the washer, you may need to give it some tugs and pulls to get it into the shape you prefer. If parts of the project need a little extra blending, you can rub the sides together, or run a fine-tooth comb over the area.
- Unfold batting and position it into a long roll. Using a long length of yarn on a metal yarn needle, baste the roll closed along the long edge and one end. Trim extra batting.
- Poke your broom handle, or dowel down into the batting towards the closed end. Push your batting through your pillow edging, making even throughout.
- Shape your edging into a doughnut, with the extra three rows at the BO end stuffed inside the co end. Stitch invisibly closed.
- Whipstitch the pillow edging to the base at the 6th row below the mice, beginning at one side of the bed bottom opening, all the way around to the other.
- Stuff the bed bottom with the rem batting. Stitch the opening closed and secure to the pillow edging. Let dry for approximately 24 hours.

Cat Toy

By Isela Phelps

A little something for your feline friend. To make it totally irresistible, stuff with a little catnip.

INTERMEDIATE

Materials

Knitting Loom

Fine gauge loom with at least 28 pegs [Sample uses DA Fine Gauge Hat Loom]

Yarn

50 yds. (45.7 m) of Aran-weight yarn
Little bits of black color yarn for eyes and nose [Sample uses Debbie Bliss Cashmerino Aran 1¾ oz (50 g) 98 yds. (90 m) 55% merino wool, 33% microfiber, 12% cashmere in light and dark gray]

Notions

Knitting tool
Tapestry needle
Row counter (optional)
Polyfil

Size(s)

About 4 ins. (10 cm) in length (does not include tail)

Gauge

5½ sts and 7 rows to 1 in. (2.5 cm)

DIRECTIONS

Cast on 28sts.
Rows 1–20: K.
Next row: K1, *k2tog; rep from * to the last st, k1.
Next 3 rows: K.
Next row: *K2tog; rep from * to the end (8 sts left).
Next row: K.
Next row: *K2tog; rep from * to the end (4sts left).

Cut yarn leaving 3 yds. (2.7 m) yarn tail to work I-cord. Thread tapestry needle through yarn tail end, and thread the last 4 sts that are on loom through the yarn tail end. Cinch them closed. With yarn coming from the cinching, seam (with mattress st) the panel lengthwise. Do not close the end yet. Stuff the body firmly with polyfil.

BO. Locate the first sts of the cast on row (the open end). Pass the tapestry needle through each of the sts (there should be 28 loops on the yarn tail). Cinch these sts close. With the rem yarn coming from the BO, work a 3-st I-cord, about 3 in. (7.5 cm) long.

Ears (Make 2)

Cast on 3 sts leaving a 10 in. (25.5 cm) beginning tail. Work a 3-st I-cord for 5 rows. Join the I-cord cast on to the BO edge. It should form a small 0.
Attach little ears to body, about one third of the way from nose tip.

Eyes and Nose

With darker gray yarn, embroider two little eyes and a nose.

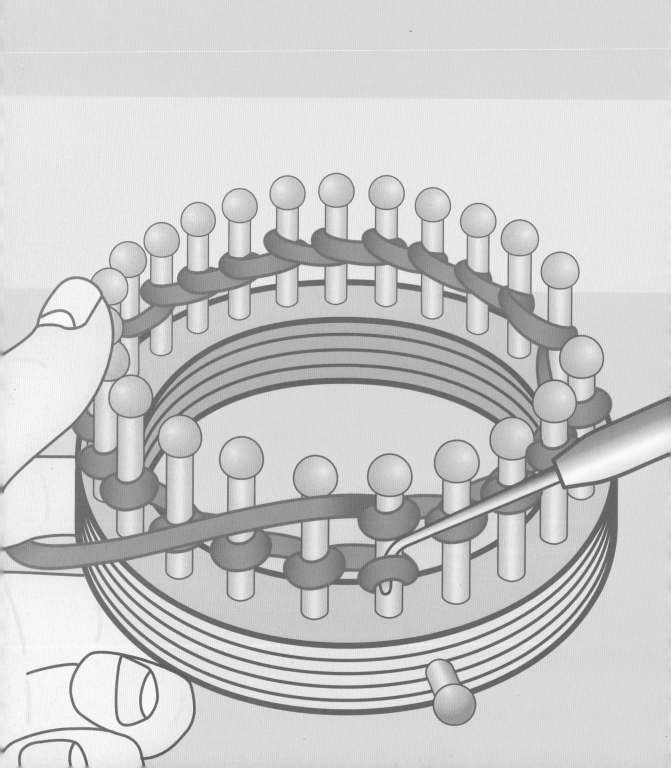

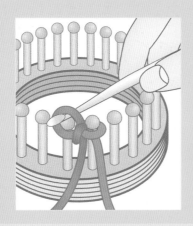

PART VI
Loom Techniques

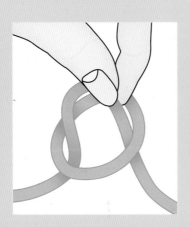

Using the Loom

In loom knitting there are two schools of thought. In needle knitting, you have the Continental and English methods—in loom knitting we have the Clockwise and Counterclockwise methods.

In the Clockwise school of thought, you will find yourself working around your knitting loom in a clockwise direction. Meaning, you will start knitting starting on the left side of the starting peg.

In the Counterclockwise school of thought, you will find yourself working around the knitting loom in a counterclockwise direction. You will begin knitting on the peg to the right of your starting peg.

Both of the methods achieve the same goal. Choose the one that feels most comfortable to you. When working on the knitting loom, it doesn't matter which way you hold the knitting loom, with pegs facing you, or opposite you, or with the loom upside down. The knitting still looks the same.

A note of warning: when reading patterns, find out in which direction the pattern is worked. If you read the pattern in the wrong direction, you will end up with a mirror image of the design.

Most of the designs in this book are worked in a clockwise direction around the knitting loom.

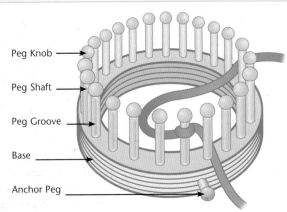

- Peg Knob
- Peg Shaft
- Peg Groove
- Base
- Anchor Peg

Loom Anatomy

There are some basic parts to the loom that you will become increasingly familiar with. This is a circular loom, but the elements are the same whether it is rake, board, or round.

Using the anchor peg

Some loom knitters prefer to use the anchor peg on their knitting loom to anchor their slip knot. This is a small peg that appears at the side of the loom. If there isn't one you can use a thumbtack to secure the slip knot. To use the anchor peg when casting on, make a slip knot leaving a 5 ins. tail. Place the slip knot on the anchor peg on the side of your knitting loom. Perform steps 2–5 as before then remove the slip knot from the anchor peg.

Slip Knot

1

Fold the circle over the working yarn that is coming from the ball.

2

Reach through the circle, and grab the yarn coming from the skein.

3

Pull the working yarn through circle, while also pulling gently on the short end of the yarn tail end, thus tightening the noose on the knot. Slip knot completed.

The E-Wrap Cast On (CO)

This cast on is called the e-wrap because if you look at it from an aerial view it resembles cursive e's. Use the e-wrap cast on when the first row needs to be picked up for a brim or seam or the cast-on row needs to be extremely flexible.

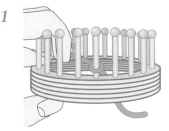

1

Place a stitch marker on any of the pegs on the knitting loom. This will be your starting peg. Make a slip knot, and place it on the peg with the stitch marker.

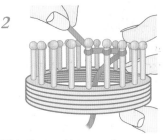

2

With the working yarn in your left hand, * pull the working yarn towards the inside of the loom, wrap around the peg directly to the left counterclockwise.
* Repeat from * to *.

Cable Cast On

1

Place a slip knot on the first peg on the loom. Take the working yarn to the outside of the loom. With a crochet hook, insert the tip of the hook through the slip knot and hook the yarn, forming a loop. Place the loop on the adjacent peg to the left.

3

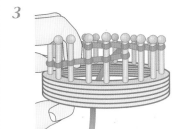

Wrap each peg a second time in the same method. Each peg should have 2 loops on it. Hold the working yarn in place so the wraps do not unravel.

4

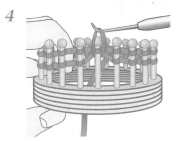

Insert the tip of knitting tool on the bottommost loop on the last peg wrapped. Lift the loop up and off the peg (knitting over, KO) and allow the loop to fall towards the inside of the knitting loom. Go to the left and repeat.

2

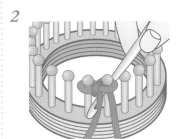

With the crochet hook go below the traveling yarn, hook the working yarn and pull towards the inside and towards the third peg. Place the loop from the hook on the next adjacent peg. Repeat this all around the loom.

3

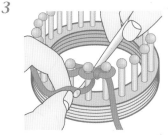

When you reach the last peg, place the loop on the first peg. The front of each peg has 2 loops, while the inside only shows 1. E-wrap the first peg with the working yarn. Knit over the 2 lowest strands, leaving only 1 loop on the peg.

4

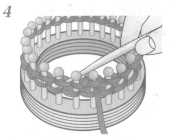

Knit over the bottommost loop on all the remaining pegs on the loom. Loom is ready to be worked in desired pattern stitch.
This creates a neat, non-loopy, thick cable-like flexible edge that is good for hats.

Chain Cast on

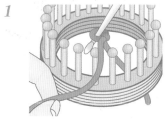

1

Form a slip knot with your yarn. Insert crochet hook through slip knot with the hook towards the center of the knitting loom and the working yarn on the outside of the loom.

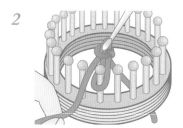

2

Place hook between first two pegs. Hook the working yarn and pull the working yarn through the slip knot that is on the crochet hook (thus, wrapping the post of the peg).

3

With crochet hook towards the inside of the loom, move up between the next set of pegs (between the second and third peg) and repeat step 2, continuing all around the loom.

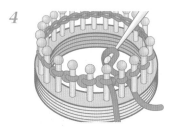

4

When you reach the last peg, take the loop on the hook and place it on the first peg. Knitting loom is ready to be knitted on.

Anchor Yarn

Place a piece of contrasting yarn in the middle of the board. The yarn is called an anchor yarn and needs to be long enough to

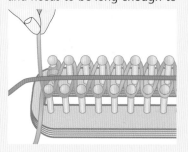

thread the ends down through the center gap of the board and tie them together, thus securing the cast-on row of stitches. The anchor yarn has two purposes:

1 It aids in pulling your item down the center of the board.
2 It helps you identify the live stitches that you will be binding off later.

Board Cast on

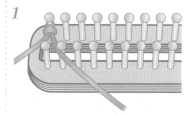

1

Make a slip knot and place it on the first top peg of the knitting board. Take working yarn down to the next peg along, and opposite, and wrap around it.

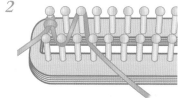

2

Go back again, missing another peg, wrap around, then down to the fourth peg, wrap around it. Continue in this manner, skipping every other peg, until you reach the end of the board (or the number of stitches you want to cover for your pattern).

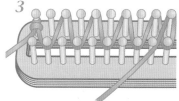

3

To complete the cast on, go to the peg directly across, wrap it. Continue wrapping the pegs that were skipped in steps 1 and 2.

Single Stitch

Single Stitch (ss)

This is the simplest stitch to get you started. Wrapping the entire loom and then knitting over may be quicker, but can create a ladder effect between the first and last peg. Also, since you are knitting in the round, if you wrap all the pegs then knit them over, your item will have a tendency to twist and you will see your vertical lines of stitches spiral around the item.

1

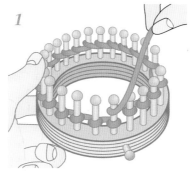

To create the single stitch, just e-wrap around all the pegs on the loom.

2

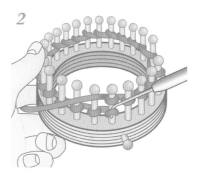

"Knit over" by lifting the bottom loop up and off the peg as shown.

Knit Stitch

1

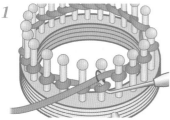

Insert the knitting tool through the stitch on the peg from bottom up.

2

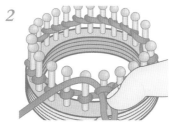

Hook the working yarn with knitting tool, making a loop. Grab the loop with your fingers.

3

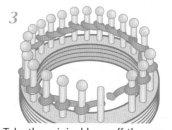

Take the original loop off the peg and replace with the new. Gently tighten the working yarn.
Repeat 1–3 to complete a knit row.

Purl Stitch

1

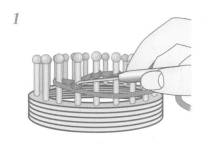

Insert the knitting tool from top to bottom through the stitch on the peg and scoop up the working yarn with the knitting tool.

2

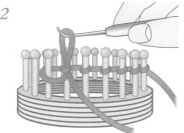

Pull the working yarn through the stitch on the peg to form a loop. Hold the new loop with your fingers.

3

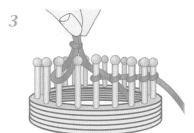

Take the old loop off the peg and place the new loop on the peg. Tug gently on the working yarn to tighten the stitch
Repeat 1–3 to complete a purl row.

The Double Stitch (ds)

This is also known as the one-over-two. The knitting loom needs to be prepped with three loops on each peg and the *bottommost* loop on the peg is lifted over and off the peg. This produces a tighter stitch than the single stitch.
It also resembles the twisted knit stitch.

1

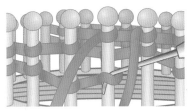

Cast on your knitting loom. E-wrap all around the knitting loom one more time. Each peg has two loops on each peg.

2

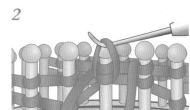

E-wrap the first peg, which now has three loops. Knit over by picking the bottonmost strand off the peg (two loops remain). Repeat step 2 all around the loom until you reach the last peg. As you move to the next peg, you may have to push down the wraps on the peg to fit the third wrap on the peg. The pegs will always have two loops after being knitted over.

The Half Stitch (hs)

The Half Stitch thus named as you have to e-wrap around the loom four times, then, knit-over two over two. It produces a thicker stitch than the double stitch. As the single stitch, and the double stitch, the knitting will resemble the twisted knit stitch. If you are knitting with a thin yarn on a large-gauge knitting loom, you may want to use the half stitch.

1

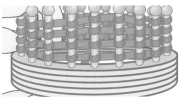

Cast on your knitting loom. E-wrap all around the knitting loom three more times. Each peg has four loops.

2

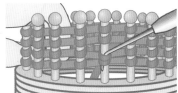

Knit over by lifting the lower two strands off the peg. Repeat all around the knitting loom. Each of the peg remains with two loops.

Chunky Braid Stitch (cbs)

This stitch resembles a knitted braid. It is also known as the three-over-one stitch, or braid stitch. It produces a thick, non-stretchy fabric with a very tight stitch. If you are knitting with a thin yarn, you may want to try this stitch throughout your project to get a firm stitch.

1

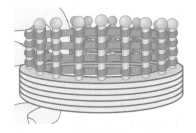

Cast on your knitting loom. E-wrap all around the knitting loom three more times. Each peg should now have four loops.

2

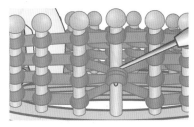

Knit over by lifting the bottonmost three loops off the peg. Repeat the knitting-over process all round the loom. The pegs remain with one loop each.

Twisted Knit Stitch

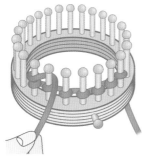

1

E-Wrap the last peg in a counterclockwise direction, run the working yarn behind to the next peg and wrap around it in a clockwise direction. Knit over this stitch, then go back and knit over on the first peg. Tug on the yarn gently to tighten the first stitch.

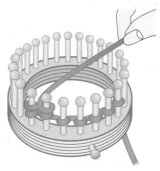

2

Continue knitting back to the next pegs in a clockwise direction. When you reach the last peg on the right, knit it, then bring working yarn to the front of the peg. Wrap around it in a clockwise direction. Bring working yarn behind the pegs.

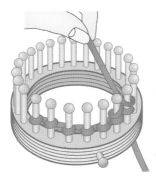

3

E-wrap the next peg in a counterclockwise direction. Knit over. Go back to the first peg and knit the stitch. Tug gently on the working yarn to tighten the first stitch.

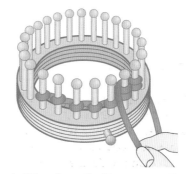

4

Continue knitting down the loom, e-wrapping the pegs in a counterclockwise direction.

Using Twisted Stitches and Mock Cables for Texture

The principle of twisting stitches to create texture consists of two stitches changing places. No special tools are necessary as it is not strictly a cable, rather a mock cable. Every time stitches are crossed over one another, the knitted item shrinks horizontally—twisting stitches makes the knitted piece narrower. Most of the time, you will encounter twisted stitch patterns on a background of reverse stockinette. The background of purl stitches helps bring out the twisted stitches and give them a three-dimensional appearance.

How to twist the stitches for right slanting: Take stitch from peg 3 off the knitting loom, hold it on your knitting tool, or on a cable needle, place it towards the center of the knitting loom. Move stitch from peg 4 to emptied peg 3. Place the stitch from the cable needle on peg 4.

How to twist the stitches for left slanting: Take stitch from peg 4 off the knitting loom, hold it on your knitting tool, or on a cable needle, place it towards the center of the knitting loom. Move stitch from peg 3 to emptied peg 4. Place the stitch from the cable needle on peg 3.

Bind Off Techniques

Used at the end of a project to cast off all the stitches, as well as when you have to bind off certain amount of stitches for buttonholes, armhole shaping, necklines, and other openings. Binding off prevents stitches from unraveling.

Basic Bind Off

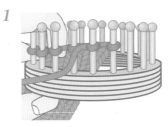

1

Knit two stitches (pegs 1 and 2).

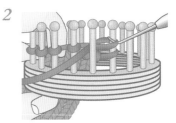

2

Move the loop from the second peg over to the first peg. Knit over.

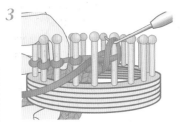

3

Move the loop on the first peg over to the peg just emptied.

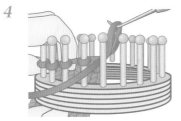

4

Knit the next peg. Repeat steps 2–4 until you have bound off the required number of stitches. A stitch will remain on the last peg. Cut the yarn leaving a long tail. E-wrap the peg and knit over—pull the tail end through the stitch.

Gather Bind Off

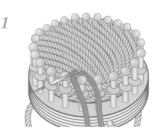

1

Cut the working yarn coming from the project, leave a 5 ins. (12 cm) tail. Or, if necessary, cut another piece of yarn that is at least 2 times the circumference of the knitting loom. Thread the yarn through a tapestry needle.

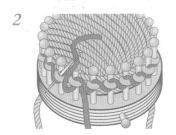

2

Pass the needle and yarn through the loop on the peg, leaving a 5 ins. tail. Continue around the loom until you reach the last peg. Pass the needle and thread through the first stitch one more time.

3

Remove the loops off the pegs. Gently pull on the beginning and end tails of the gathering yarn. Continue pulling on the tail ends until the top of the item is closed. Use the tapestry needle to sew the hole closed.

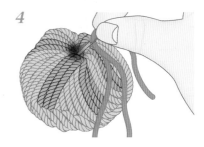

4

Grab the yarn tail end coming from the knitting of the hat. Tie the three strands (the two ends from the gathering yarn and the one from the knitting of the hat) together. Make a square knot and weave in the ends.

Yarn Over Bind Off

The yarn over bind off provides a stretchy border, perfect for items that require a flexible opening like magic scarves, ruffles, or leggings.

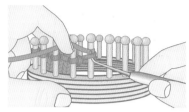

Knit the first stitch. (Peg 1).

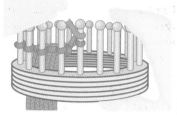

Wrap the peg in a clockwise direction, knit over.

Knit the next stitch (Peg 2).

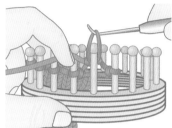

Move the stitch over (from peg 2 to peg 1) to the peg on the left. KO. Repeat 2–4 until all the stitches required have been bound off. A stitch will remain on the last peg. Cut the working yarn leaving a 5-ins. (12 cm) tail. E-wrap the peg and knit over—pull the tail end through the stitch.

Sewn Bind Off

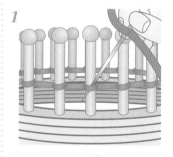

Pass the needle through the first stitch by inserting the needle from top to bottom.

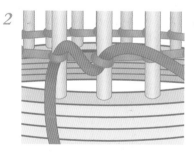

Pass the needle through the second stitch by inserting the needle from top to bottom.

Insert the needle through the first stitch by inserting the needle from bottom to top.

Take the stitch off the peg. Repeat 1–4 until there is only one stitch on the loom. Pass the needle through the stitch from bottom to top. Take stitch off the peg.

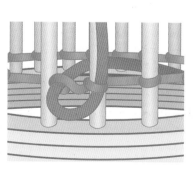

Single Crochet Bind Off

1

Remove a stitch from the peg with the hook (2 loops on hook). Wrap the working yarn round the crochet hook.

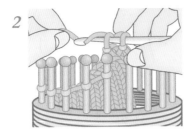

2

Pull the yarn through the loops on the hook to make another loop.

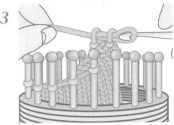

3

Move to the next peg and repeat 1–2. When you reach the last stitch, cut the working yarn leaving a 5 ins. (12 cm) tail, hook the tail and pass it through the last stitch to lock it in place.

Double Crochet Bind Off

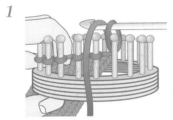

1

Hook the working yarn with the crochet hook; pull the yarn through the stitch on the hook to make a loop.

2

Make 1 chain (crochet 1 chain). Move to the next peg and repeat steps 1–2.

3

When you reach the last stitch, cut the working yarn leaving a 5 ins. (12 cm) tail, hook the tail and pass it through the last stitch to fasten off.

Joining Two Panels

1

Place one of the panels on the knitting loom with the right side facing the inside of the knitting loom; the wrong side will be facing you. Pay close attention to putting the stitches back on the knitting loom correctly.

2

Place the second panel on the knitting loom by placing the stitches on the same pegs that the first panel is occupying, right sides of the panels together. Follow the Basic Bind Off method and bind off the stitches—knit through both stitches on the pegs

3

Take the two stitches off the peg and place the newly formed loop on the peg. Once you get the hang of this, your seams will be invisible.

Three-needle Bind Off

1

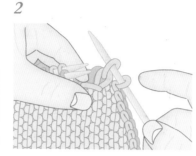

With one panel on one needle, and the other panel on another needle:Insert the third knitting needle through both first stitches and knit them together.

2

Repeat with the next set of two stitches.

3

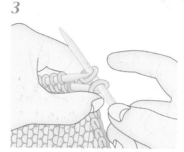

Pass the first stitch on the right knitting needle over the second stitch—1 stitch bound off.

Grafting

This provides a seamless join, perfect for socks. You will need 2 knitting needles, size 8 (5 mm) when knitting with thick yarns, or size 2 (2.75 mm) when knitting with thin yarns. Hold the needles parallel with the tips pointing in the same direction, wrong sides facing each other.

Caution: Be sure that the stitches are set up on the needles correctly. The stitches should sit exactly as in diagram 1.

• Begin by inserting the tapestry needle into the first stitch on the needle closest to you as if to purl (from right to left, diagram 2), pull through, leave stitch on the needle.
• Insert the needle into the first stitch on the back needle as if to knit (from left to right), leave the stitch on the needle. Pull the yarn through.
• Insert the needle into the first stitch on the front needle as if to knit. Slip stitch off the needle.

1

2

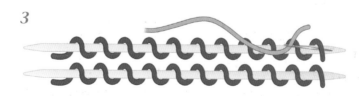

3

• Insert the needle into the next stitch on the front needle as if to purl. Leave stitch on the needle. Gently pull on the working yarn to snug up the stitch. Do not pull too much.

• Insert the needle into the first stitch on the back needle as if to purl, and slip it off the needle.
• Continue working back and forth, pulling gently on the working yarn to keep an even tension.

Finishing Off the Cast-On Edge

The anchor yarn is holding the first loops as "live" stitches. When the project is completed, the cast-on edge needs to be finished by crocheting. The following steps will show how to accomplish this essential step of the knitted garment. In order to finish the "live" stitches, you need to have a crochet hook that will work with the weight yarn used.

1

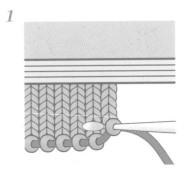

Insert crochet hook in the first stitch.

2

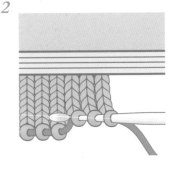

Insert the hook through the next two stitches.

3

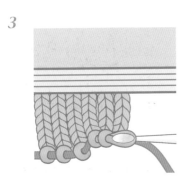

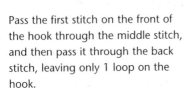

Pass the first stitch on the front of the hook through the middle stitch, and then pass it through the back stitch, leaving only 1 loop on the hook.

4

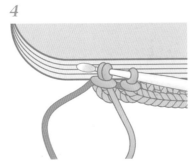

Repeat steps 2 and 3 with the remaining stitches. When you reach the end, form a chain with the yarn tail end and pass it through the last loop. After all the stitches have been bound off with the crochet hook, you can remove the anchor yarn by pulling it out.

Weaving the Tail Ends

You have finished your first project, it is almost ready to be worn, but you still need to hide those unsightly tail ends from your yarn. What to do? It is fairly simple: all you need is a large tapestry needle. To hide the unsightly yarn tail ends work on the wrong side of the item.

1

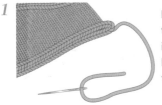

Locate the yarn tail end; thread it through the large eye of a tapestry needle.

2

Working on the wrong side of the item weave the yarn tail end about 1 ins. (2.5 cm) in one direction by inserting the needle through the "bump" of each knit stitch. Go up/down one row weaving in for about an ins.

Steps 1–2 should create a "Z" with the tail end. Cut the remainder of the yarn as close to the knitted item as possible. Repeat this process with each yarn tail end you have in your knitted item.

Increases (inc)

This is adding extra stitches to the panel, thus making it wider. When increases happen within rows, it is recommended to only increase 2 stitches on a given row. Increases are used to shape items such as sweater sleeves, skirts, and items that fan out. There are various ways to increase stitches on the loom, and all of them require you to move the stitches outwards to the empty pegs to allow room, or an empty peg, for the new stitch. Below, you will find three methods. Familiarize yourself with all three of them.

Decreases (dec)

Removing stitches from your panel will make the panel narrower. When decreases happen within rows, try to decrease 1 or 2 stitches in from either edge to keep the selvedge neat. There are various ways to decrease on the knitting loom; all of them require you to move the stitches inward. Familiarize yourself with the methods below.

Make 1 (M1)

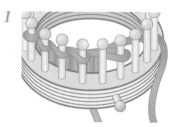
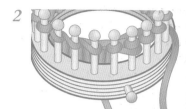

1 Move the last stitch to the next empty peg outward, leaving an empty peg between the last peg and the peg before last.

2 Make 1 (M1). Knit the stitches on the knitting loom: when you reach the empty peg, e-wrap it and continue knitting to the end of the row. Increasing in this manner will leave a small hole where the increase was created.

Lifted Increase Make 1

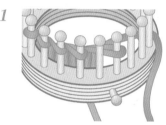
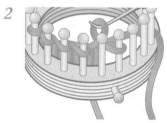

1 Move the last stitch to the next empty peg outwards leaving an empty peg between the last peg and the peg before last.

2 With the knitting tool reach for the running-ladder coming from the two stitches on either side below the empty peg. Twist the strand and place it on the empty peg (if you don't twist it, you will create a small hole). Knit your row as usual.

Knit 2-Together

Knitting 2 together (k2tog) creates a right slanting decrease, and is best created at the beginning of a knit row.

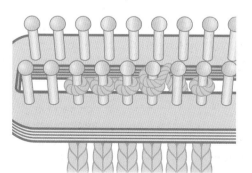

Slip, Slip Knit

The left slanting decrease is the mirror image of a k2tog and is achieved by a Slip, Slip Knit (ssk) at the end of a row.

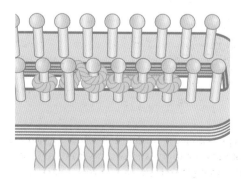

Short Row Shaping

This allows shaping a knitted panel without the aid of increasing stitches. It creates soft curves by knitting a row to a certain stitch in the row, then turning back and knitting in the other direction. It is a method commonly used in heels, blouse darts for the stomach or bust area, and in any other item where you want seamless curves.

Shaping with short-rows has one pitfall that you must be aware of. It is necessary to wrap the stitch after the turning point to avoid a hole between the turning stitch and the next stitch. The "wrap" eliminates the hole almost completely.

How to Wrap and Turn (W&T)

When knitting each wrapped peg, lift both the wrap and the stitch together, 2 over 1, as this will eliminate the wrap and fill the hole made with the short rows.

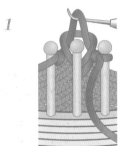

1

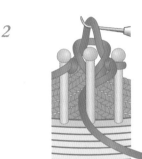

2

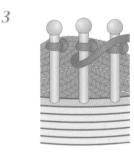

3

Knit or purl to the desired turning stitch. Take the stitch off the next peg and hold it with your knitting tool.

Wrap the peg by taking the yarn towards the inside of the loom and wrapping around the peg. The working yarn will end up to the front of the knitting loom.

Place the stitch back on the peg. Take working yarn and knit or purl back across the row.

Knitting Board Shaping

Increasing: recommended use when casting on more than 2 stitches.

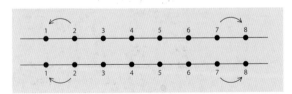

To increase the numbers of stitches, simply Figure-8-wrap the next set of empty pegs twice. Wrap the other pegs so that the entire board has 2 loops on each peg. Knit over as usual.

This type of increase method leaves a step edge. For a gradual increase, try the next method.

For example, the knitting board above has stitches from pegs 2–7. Increase at peg 8 by figure-8-wrapping peg 8A and 8B twice. Increase on the other side by Figure-8-wrapping peg 1A and 1B twice.

Decreasing: Use this at the very end/beginning of a row.

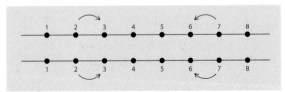

Dec: The decrease is similar to the increase method with the exception that the stitches need to move towards the center of the board. The pegs adjacent to the decrease will have an extra stitch.

1 Move the last stitches inwards to the adjacent peg.

2 Wrap and knit over. Make sure to knit over 2 over 1 on the pegs with the extra stitches.

3-Stitch I-cord

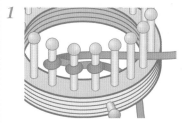

1 Cast on 3 pegs. With working yarn coming from the third peg run the yarn behind the pegs to the first peg.

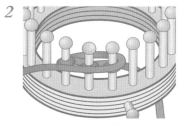

2 Bring yarn to the front of the loom and knit the 3 pegs.

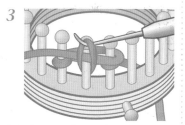

3 Knit the second peg, then the first, and the third last.
Repeat steps until the cord measures the desired length.

Mattress Stitch

1 Lay the pieces to be joined, right side up and side-by-side. Thread a tapestry needle with the tail end. Bring the yarn through to the front, in the middle of the first stitch on the first row of the seam. Take the needle through to the same position on the other piece, and bring it out in the middle of the edge stitch one row up.

2 Insert the needle back into the first piece of fabric, in the same place that the yarn last came out. Then bring the needle out in the middle of the stitch above. Repeat this making a zig-zag seam from edge to edge for a few more rows. You can pull the thread firmly, and the stitches almost disappear. When the seam is finished, weave in the ends.

4-st LC (4-st Left Cross Cable)

A left cross 4 stitch cable takes place over 4 stitches, on pegs 1–4.
1 Skip first two stitches (stitches on pegs 1 and 2).
2 Knit the next 2 stitches (stitches on pegs 3 and 4), slip these two stitches to a cable needle, and hold at the back of work.

3 Knit the stitches skipped on step 1 (stitches on pegs 1 and 2). Place these stitches on empty pegs (place stitch from peg 1 on peg 3 and stitch from peg 2 on peg 4).
4 Take the stitches from the cable needle and place them on the two remaining pegs (pegs 1 and 2).
5 Gently, pull on the stitch on peg 3 and then the stitch on peg 4 to tighten the stitches.

4-st RC (4-st Right Cross Cable)

A right cross 4 stitch cable; takes place over 4 stitches, on pegs 1–4.
1 Take stitches off peg 1 and 2 and place them on cable needle.
2 Knit peg 3. Place it on peg 1.
3 Knit peg 4. Place it on peg 2.
4 Take stitch 1 from cable needle and place it on peg 3. Knit it.
5 Take stitch 2 from cable needle and place it on peg 4. Knit it.

Lazy Daisy instructions:

1 Thread tapestry needle with CC. Bring needle up at inner point of petal where you want the first petal.
2 Form a loop with the working yarn, push the needle back down through the same inner point. Maintain the loop shape.
3 Insert the needle so that it pops out by the loop end (inside the petal).
4 Cross over the loop and insert the needle down, pull gently on the working yarn. This loop will secure the daisy petal.
The above forms one petal; repeat instructions to form more petals. Each daisy has five petals.

Quick Reference

Large Gauge knitting looms

- Distance from center of peg to center of peg: ¾ ins. (2 cm)
- **Available in:** wood & plastic, with nylon pegs, plastic, wood, and metal
- **Yarn:** Bulky-weight yarns or 2 strands of medium-weight yarn
- **Knits:** Bulky-weight knits and knits that will be felted
- **Loom Gauge:** Approximately 1½–2 stitches per 1 in. (2.5 cm)
- Compared to needle knitting stitch gauge: size 13 (9 mm)

Regular Gauge Knitting Looms

- Distance from center of peg to center of peg: ½ in. (1.2 cm)
- **Available in:** wood & plastic, with nylon pegs, plastic, wood, and metal
- **Yarn:** Chunky-weight yarns or 2 strands of sport-weight yarn
- **Knits:** Medium-weight knits
- **Gauge:** Approximately 3–3.5 stitches per 1 in. (2.5 cm)
- Compared to needle knitting stitch gauge: size 10 (6 mm)

Small Gauge Knitting Looms

- Distance from center of peg to center of peg: 3/8 to 3/7 ins.
- **Available in:** wood & plastic, with nylon pegs, plastic, wood, and metal
- **Yarn:** Worsted-weight/medium-weight yarn
- **Knits:** Medium and light weight knits
- **Gauge:** Approximately 3.5–4 stitches per 1 in. (2.5 cm)
- Compared to needle knitting stitch gauge: size 7–8 (4.5–5 mm)

Fine Gauge Knitting Looms

- Distance from center of peg to center of peg: ¼ ins.
- **Available in:** wood base and metal pins/pegs
- **Yarn:** Sports-weight/DK-weight
- **Knits:** Light-weight knits
- **Gauge:** Approximately 4–5 stitches per 1 in. (2.5 cm)
- Compared to needle knitting stitch Gauge: Size 5–6 (3.75–4 mm)

Extra Fine Gauge Knitting Looms

- Distance from center of peg to center of peg: 3/16 ins.
- **Available in:** wood base and metal pins/pegs
- **Yarn:** Fingering-weight/sock-weight
- **Knits:** Light-weight knits
- **Gauge:** Approximately 7–8 stitches per 1 in. (2.5 cm)
- Compared to needle knitting stitch gauge: size 1.5–2 (2.25–2.75 mm)

Yarn Weight Symbol	1 SUPER FINE	2 FINE	3 LIGHT	4 MEDIUM	5 BULKY	6 SUPER BULKY
Types of Yarn	Sock, Fingering, Baby Weight	Sport, Baby	DK Light, Worsted	Worsted, Aran	Chunky	Bulky
Knit Gauge in Stockinette Stitch per ins.	7–8	5–6	4–5	3–4	2–3	1½–2
Recommended Knitting loom Gauge	Extra-Fine Gauge	Fine Gauge	Small Gauge	Regular Gauge	Regular/ Large Gauge	Large Gauge

Yarn Recommended	1 SUPER FINE	2 FINE	3 LIGHT	4 MEDIUM	5 BULKY	6 SUPER BULKY
Distance from center of pin to center of pin in inches	3/16	1/4	3/8–3/7	1/2	5/8–3/4	4/5
Loom Gauge	Extra Fine Gauge	Fine Gauge	Small Gauge	Regular Gauge	Large Gauge	Large Gauge
Manufacturers	Décor Accents	Décor Accents	Décor Accents	Knifty Knitter Long Series Décor Accents	Knifty Knitters Décor Accents	Knifty Knitters

Common Abbreviations Found in Loom Knitting

[ ]	work instructions in brackets as many times as directed
( )	work instructions in parentheses in the place directed
* *	repeat instructions between the asterisks as directed
*	repeat instructions following the single asterisk as directed
"	denotes inches
alt	alternate
approx	approximately
b	bobble
bc	back cross
beg	begin/beginning
bet or btw	between
BO	bind off
but	buttonhole
CA	color a
cab	cable
CB	color b
cbs	chunky braid stitch
cc	contrasting color
cdc	central double decrease
ch	chain (use a crochet hook)
cm	denotes centimeters
cn	cable needle
co	cast on
col	color
cont	continue
cr L	cross left
cr R	cross right
dbl	double
dec	decrease
diam	diameter

ds	double stitch
ew	e-wrap
foll	follow/following
fc	front cross
fs	flat stitch/knit stitch
g	denotes grams
g st	garter stitch
hs	half stitch
inc	increase
K or k	knit
kbl	knit through back of loop. In looming this is created by e-wrap
k2tog	knit 2 together—creates a right-slanting decrease.
l	left
lc	left cross
lp(s)	loop(s)
Lt	left twist
m	denotes meters
mb	make bobble
m1	make one—increase one stitch
MC	main color
mm	denotes millimeters
mul	multiple
oz	denotes ounces
P or p	purl
p2tog	purl 2 stitches together—creates a right-slanting decrease
pm	place marker
prev	previous
psso	pass slipped stitch over
rc	right cross
rem	remaining/remain
rep	repeat
rev St st	reverse stockinette stitch
rnd(s)	round(s)

rs	right side
rt	right twist
sc	single crochet
sel	selvedge
sk	skip
skn	skein
skp	slip, knit, pass stitch over—creates a decrease
sl	slip
sl st	slip stitch
ss	single stitch
ssk	slip, slip, knit these two stitches together—creates a left-slanting decrease
ssp	slip, slip, purl these two stitches together—creates a left-slanting decrease
st(s)	stitch (es)
St st	stockinette stitch (knit every row)
tog	together
tw or tw	twist stitches for a mock cable
wy	working yarn
yd(s)	denotes yards
yo	yarn over
zip	zipper

Useful Information

Reading charts

Charts are pictorial representations of stitch patterns, color patterns, or shaping patterns. Reading charts in loom knitting differs from reading a chart when needle knitting. In needle knitting, the knitting is turned after every row, exposing the wrong and right side of the fabric every other row. In loom knitting, the right side of the fabric is always in front, so we follow the pictorial chart as it appears.

- Charts are visual and pictorial representations of the stitch pattern. A chart allows you to see the entire stitch pattern.
- Charts are numbered on both sides, even numbers on the right side, odd on the left.
- Start reading the chart on the bottom.
- Each square represents a stitch.
- Each horizontal row of squares represents a row.
- Stitch-pattern charts use symbols to represent stitches such as knit, purl, twists, yarn-overs, and any other stitch manipulation needed.
- Thick black lines represent the end of a pattern stitch repeat. The stitches after the black line are edge, or selvedge, stitches.
- Charts for color knitting differ from stitch-pattern charts. In color pattern charts each different color square represents the color needed on that particular stitch.

- For Circular Knitting: read the chart from bottom up from right to left.
- For Flat Knitting: read the chart from bottom up from right to left on odd rows, and from left to right on even rows.
- Remember: the right side of the knitted fabric is always facing the outside. Knit the stitches as they appear on the chart.

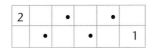

Chart Key

P Purl •

K Knit ☐

Chart reads:

For Flat Knitting:

Row 1: k1, p1, k1, p1
Row 2: k1, p1, k1, p1

For Circular Knitting:

Round 1: *k1, p1, rep from * to the end
Round 2: *p1, k1, rep from * to the end

A complete list of chart symbols and abbreviations used in this book is provided in the index section (we are using needle knitting standard abbreviations and symbols whenever possible).

Washing your knits

Hand-washing is the best washing technique for all your knitted items. Even those items that were knitted with machine-washable yarns can have their life extended by practicing good washing habits.

Use pure soap flakes or special wool soap. Wash and rinse your item gently in warm water. Maintain an even water temperature; changing water temperature can shock your wool items and accidentally felt them. Before washing, test for colorfastness. If the yarn bleeds, wash the item in cold water. If the yarn is colorfast, wash with warm water.

Fill a basin or sink with water, add the soap flakes or wool soap, and using your hands, gently wash the knitted item. Avoid rubbing, unless you want your item to matt the yarn and felt it together.

To rinse, empty the basin and fill with clean warm water, immerse your knitted item and gently squeeze out all the soap suds. Repeat until all the soap suds are gone and the water is soap free. Pat as much of the water out as you can; use the palms of your hands. Do not wring your item as this may cause wrinkles and distort the yarn. Place the knitted item between two towels and squeeze as much of the water out as you can.

To dry your item, lay it flat away from direct sunlight; block again if necessary to match measurements.

Resources

Knitting Looms

The knitting looms used in this book were provided by two vendors, Décor Accents, Inc., and Provo Craft. If you would like to find a larger variety do an internet search for knitting looms or loom knitting and you will find a larger selection at your fingertips.

Décor Accents, Inc.
www.dalooms.com
P.O. Box 549
Newton, UT 84327

Provo Craft
www.provocraft.com
151 East 3450 North
Spanish Fork, UT 84660

Blocking wires available from:
Take it Personally
www.giftsbytip.com

Yarns

Berroco, Inc.
14 Elmdale Rd.
PO Box 367
Uxbridge, MA 01569
info@berroco.com
www.berroco.com

Brown Sheep Yarn Company
10062 County Road 16
Mitchell, NE 69357

Crystal Palace Yarns
160 23rd St
Richmond, CA 94804
www.straw.com

Joann.com
2361 Rosecrans Ave
El Segundo, CA 90245
www.joann.com

Knitting Fever, Inc.
P.O. Box 502
Roosevelt, NY 11575
www.knittingfever.com
(Distributors of Rowan, Debbie Bliss, and Sublime yarns)

Koigu Wool Designs
RR #1
Williamsford, ON N0H 2V0
Canada
info@koigu.com

Lion Brand Yarns
135 Kero Road
Carlstadt, NJ 07072
www.lionbrand.com

Manos del Uruguay
www.rosiesyarncellar.com

Misti Alpaca
P.O. Box 2532
Glen Ellyn, IL 60138
www.mistialpaca.com

Muench Yarns
285 Bel Marin Keys Blvd
Unit J
Novata, CA 94949
www.muenchyarns.com

Patons
PO Box 40
Listowel, ON N4W 3H3
Canada
www.patonsyarns.com

Plymouth Yarn Co.
PO Box 28
Bristol, PA 19007
pyc@plymouthyarn.com
www.plymouthyarn.com

Tahki Stacy Charles, Inc.
70–30 80th St. Building 36
Ridgewood, NY 11385
info@tahkistacycharles.com
1.800.338.YARN, Inc.

GGH
Distributed by Muench Yarns:
1323 Scott Street
Petaluma, CA 94954-1135
info@muenchyarns.com

Louet
3425 Hands Rd,
Prescott, ON K0E 1T0
Canada
www.louet.com

Contributors

Tracey Carsto

Easy Lacy Socks

Tracey has been crafting in one form or another since she was six years old. She has always loved the look of knitted garments, especially socks, but found it hard to produce with needles. One day she saw a knitting loom in a store and she was hooked. Soon she was looking for smaller gauge looms and she found sock looms. Since there were no pattern books out then, she naturally started designing her own sock patterns. She blogs at http://traceycarsto.blogspot.com/

Bethany Dailey

Magic Tween Top, Cat Cozy, Pooch Parka

Bethany has loved crafting her entire life, but for the last three years, her passion has been loom knitting. She enjoys creating original loom knitting designs and sharing her interest with others through her local craft store, her city college, and her blog, Gettin' It Pegged~Loom Knitter's Clique. Bethany shares a home in Southwest Washington with her husband and two daughters. You can find out all about her latest projects and patterns, and her life, at www.GettinItPegged.com.

Denise Layman

Rosette Cardigan, Sailboat Cardigan, Baby Bunting

Denise first picked up a knitting loom about five years ago and has been designing loom knitting patterns for about three years. She is the author of *Learn to Knit on Circle Looms*, and is also the co-editor of *Loom Knitters Circle*, an online loom-knitting magazine.

Denise has a degree in education, and uses it to home-school her four young children.

Evelyn H. Monsay

Cable & Ribs Socks

Evelyn learned about a broad spectrum of fiber arts at a very young age from her mother. Her introduction to loom knitting was with a spool knitter at that time, and her interest was recently rekindled with the discovery of the extra-fine gauge looms produced by Décor Accents. Her "other" life includes a career as a photonics engineer, technology program manager, and most recently (for fifteen years) a physics professor. Her other interests include book arts, glassblowing and flameworking, dollmaking, ballet, and freestyle skating. She lives with her husband and family of cats in central New York.

Kathy Norris

Spice, Sugar, A Touch of Lace, Pi Sweater, Fun Animal Hats, Bonnets & Matching Bootees.

Kathy started her career as a designer at the young age of ten when she made clothes for her dolls. A passion for fiber arts developed when she picked up knitting needles over twenty-five years ago. This passion was extended to loom knitting six years ago. In addition to designing, Kathy teaches knitting and loom knitting in Antelope Valley, California where she resides with her family and yarn stash.

Isela Phelps

Everything else

A fiber lover by day and night, Isela Phelps has been involved in

fiber arts from an early age. She began loom knitting about seven years ago and since then she has been an integral part of the loom knitting community. She has launched various online websites to help spread the word about loom knitting, one of which is an online magazine focused on loom knitting, Loom Knitters Circle, found at www.loomknitterscircle.com, where she serves as an editor.

She has appeared on national television on the popular *Knitty Gritty* show, a Do-It-Yourself Network production, where she demonstrated the use of a knitting loom to the world. Her designs and articles can be found in books, and online, and in major magazines. Isela lives with her family in Cache Valley, Utah. For more information, check out her blog at: www.purlingsprite.com.

Stacey Sobiesiak

Cascading Shawl, Hat and Scarf Set

Stacey lives and works in the High Desert of Southern California. A native Pennsylvanian, surprisingly, she did not learn to knit and spin until moving to a warmer climate. An unfortunate accident in 2006 left her unable to play with fiber for several months. A friend sent her several looms and a new obsession was born. Already an accomplished creator of hand-painted embroidery canvases, she began designing loom and knit patterns soon after. In her fiber-free time, she works in a safety office, owns a small business, is working towards a degree in History and tries to keep up with her blog "Purling Dervish". (www.purlingdervishes.com/blog).

Index

Index

Dedicated: To my Abuelita Delfina who
shared with me her love of the fiber arts.

Acknowledgments

I would like to thank everyone involved in helping me create this book.
To my sample knitters: Jennifer Stark, Liz Anderson, Stephanie McElheran.
Without their help many of the projects in this book would not have been
possible. To the contributors: Kathy Norris, Denise Layman, Bethany Dailey,
Evelyn Monsay, Tracey Carsto, and Stacey Sobiesiak; for their great designs
and for sharing their creative talent.

A heartfelt thank you to Katy Bevan, my editor, for her invaluable help in
editing the various sections of the book. For her patience, encouragement,
and guidance throughout the workload of the book.

To the different yarn companies that provided yarn for the projects:
Louet, Debbie Bliss, Sublime, Berroco, and Blue Sky Alpacas: thank you for
providing the fiber fix.

A bucketful of gratitude to all the models, especially Katy's kitty cat who
came to the rescue at the last minute to model the Cat Cozy Bed.

Lastly, a thank you to all of you, my loom-knitting friends, for making the
first book a success, and for your support while making the second one.

Quintet Publishing would like to thank the models featured throughout the
book: Margot de Naurois, Katie Everitt, Josh Everitt, Mia Haggi, Sean Hart,
Charlotte Linton, and Snappy with his handler Teresa de Perignat.